New Directions for
Adult and Continuing
Education

Susan Imel
Jovita M. Ross-Gordon
COEDITORS-IN-CHIEF

Challenging
Homophobia
and Heterosexism

Lesbian, Gay, Bisexual, Transgender, and Queer Issues in Organizational Settings

Robert J. Hill

EDITOR

Number 112 • Winter 2006
Jossey-Bass
San Francisco

CHALLENGING HOMOPHOBIA AND HETEROSEXISM
Robert J. Hill (ed.)
New Directions for Adult and Continuing Education, no. 112
Susan Imel, Jovita M. Ross-Gordon, Coeditors-in-Chief

Microfilm copies of issues and articles are available in 16mm and 35mm, as well as microfiche in 105mm, through University Microfilms Inc., 300 North Zeeb Road, Ann Arbor, Michigan 48106-1346.

NEW DIRECTIONS FOR ADULT AND CONTINUING EDUCATION (ISSN 1052-2891, electronic ISSN 1536-0717) is part of The Jossey-Bass Higher and Adult Education Series and is published quarterly by Wiley Subscription Services, Inc., A Wiley Company, at Jossey-Bass, 989 Market Street, San Francisco, California 94103-1741. Periodicals Postage Paid at San Francisco, California, and at additional mailing offices. POSTMASTER: Send address changes to New Directions for Adult and Continuing Education, Jossey-Bass, 989 Market Street, San Francisco, California 94103-1741.

SUBSCRIPTIONS cost $80.00 for individuals and $195.00 for institutions, agencies, and libraries.

EDITORIAL CORRESPONDENCE should be sent to the Coeditors-in-Chief, Susan Imel, ERIC/ACVE, 1900 Kenny Road, Columbus, Ohio 43210-1090, e-mail: imel.l@osu.edu; or Jovita M. Ross-Gordon, Southwest Texas State University, EAPS Dept., 601 University Drive, San Marcos, TX 78666.

Cover photograph by Jack Hollingsworth@Photodisc

www.josseybass.com

Contents

EDITOR'S NOTES

Challenging Homophobia and Heterosexism is about examining and improving adult and continuing education practice within lesbian, gay, bisexual, transgender, and queer (LGBTQ) discourses. There is a pressing need for such a volume since people in many professional settings—schools, colleges and universities, businesses, corporations, social institutions, nonprofits, government units, and civil society and nongovernment organizations—wrestle with issues surrounding sexual minorities. A common goal of the chapters in this volume is to help professionals to better understand the lived experiences of LGBTQ people. Our hope is that readers will recognize the legitimacy of sexual minority concerns in learning across the life span. This volume is intended to capture the personal, social, and legal consequences that may result from avoiding issues of same-sex sexual orientation, gender identity, and gender expression in professional environments. It will allow professionals to better respond to critical incidents of antigay behavior and construct social, public, and organizational policies to create inclusive and safe work and learning environments. These chapters detail the many ways that adult and continuing education and workforce training inform opinions and foster conversations for LGBTQ justice within organizations.

Chapters in this volume work together to weave a tapestry of many hues. In Chapter One, Robert J. Hill presents a synopsis of LGBTQ issues in adult and continuing education, and argues that organizations are key players in sexual minority discourses. The title of his chapter, "What's It Like to Be Queer Here?" is an inevitable question, given the pervasive nature of organizations on the landscape and the growing number of "out" sexual minorities that are a part of them. This chapter proceeds from the perspective of the LGBTQ organizational member, often a worker or volunteer in the public or private setting. It also looks specifically at the history of LGBTQ issues in adult and continuing education. Chapter Eight is the other bookend to the volume, bracketing a host of queer discussions from multiple perspectives. It proceeds from the vantage point of human resource managers.

Chapters Two and Three focus on development, that is, achieving improved well-being. Chapter Two, by Kathleen P. King and Susan C. Biro, explores sexual identity development. It presents a unique and dynamic LGBTQ transformative learning model that blends Mezirow's stages (1991) with a sexual orientation–sexual identity schema to create an interactive process of shifting and framing perspectives. Chapter Three, by Tonette S. Rocco and Suzanne J. Gallagher, examines career development. It asks, "How can we create nondiscriminatory—and queer—work environments

WILEY
InterScience®
DISCOVER SOMETHING GREAT

for heterosexual and LGBTQ people?" It reminds us that this will require interventions at the individual, program, and advocacy levels.

Chapter Four, by Julie Gedro, teases out experiences of lesbians in organizational settings where double bias can be encountered. It is here that the confluence of gender and sexual orientation creates barriers to advancement. Gedro presents various development models and confronts organizational heterosexism and homophobia from the lens of lesbian discursive practice, a highly neglected frame in adult and continuing education.

Chapter Five, by André P. Grace and Kristopher Wells, and Chapter Six, by Thomas V. Bettinger, Rebecca Timmins, and Elizabeth J. Tisdell, direct readers specifically to educational settings. In Chapter Five, preservice and continuing teacher professional development are unpacked, and Chapter Six looks at higher education. In the latter, Bettinger and Timmins, both graduate students of adult education, self-report on their experiences as sexual minorities in academe; Tisdell, a faculty member, challenges readers to think about the fluid nature of one's sexual orientation and how that affects the classroom. Both chapters juxtapose "solutions" at the personal and the institutional level.

Chapter Seven, by Eunice Ellen Hornsby, is evolutionary in a number of respects. It picks up where several of the preceding chapters end, that is, how to use policy to drive organizational change, and it lays out the evolving nature and trends of law and policy. In a practical way, it offers a checklist for people engaged in policy development that will help to sensitize individuals to the discriminatory effects of ill-conceived policies. Hornsby offers some international perspectives, as does the work by Grace and Wells (largely in a Canadian context) in Chapter Five.

Chapter Eight, by Corey S. Muñoz and Kecia M. Thomas, is a lucid presentation of best practices for LGBTQ inclusion in organizations. Like Chapter Five, it presents strategies for navigating homophobia and heterosexism—the former in business settings and the latter in education. All four authors confront unsympathetic workplaces and offer insights into optimum ways to dampen hostility. Finally, Chapter Nine by Hill summarizes the issues by pulling together some common themes found in the volume.

In one way or another, all authors note the cultural war raging over sexual orientation and gender expression in society and the consequences that this has on individuals' lives, including life in organizational settings—and especially at work. It is a snapshot of a major issue that is complex, contested, resisted, and evolving.

Some Thoughts About Language

A brief detour into the language employed in this volume is in order. Language is not transparent; it does not simply communicate reality in an innocent or direct way that links a word to an object (see Lather, 1996). Language helps to construct, privilege, or marginalize. This, of course, makes problematic any definitions provided here. Labels not only describe; they inscribe people. Terms that may be considered problematic are used throughout this volume and include *gay, lesbian, straight, bisexual, transgender, transsexual, transidentified, transphobia, queer, homosexual, homophobia, heteronormative,* and several more. The following thoughts are offered in order to better understand the ways that authors employ (and deploy) some of these terms.

Homosexual and *homosexuality* are clinical words based in a psychologistic model and have limited capacity to describe the range of personal being and behaving. Ragins (2004), who presents comprehensible explanations of a number of sexual terms, reports that these "constructions are quite complex and are infused with social and political influences" (p. 37). Some of these influences emerge in this volume.

It is important from the outset to distinguish between *sexual orientation* and *gender identity*. Notions of sexual orientation (that is, mobilized sexual and affectional desires) have changed considerably over the past half-century. The binary *gay* (homosexual) and *straight* (heterosexual), with bisexuality the center point, is heavily contested and no longer seems adequate. "Sexual categories have become conceptually and ideologically suspect. . . . Lesbian, gay, and feminist theorists have repeatedly contested the essential, intrinsic, or universal character of sexual identities" (Hostetler and Herdt, 1998, p. 249). Situating gender and sexual categories as immutable, unimpeachable, timeless, and purely descriptive is an essentialist myth of epistemological theories of justification. Binaries limit our thinking about gender and sexual orientation; the notion of a unitary and coherent straight, gay, lesbian, or bisexual subject may well be a fantasy. A much more elaborate analysis points to the fact that "same-sex" behavior may not lead to a "gay" self-identity and that there are vastly individual differences in the development of orientations and gender identities. The recent construction of African American men "on the down low" (or "dl," that is, engaging in veiled same-sex behavior while publicly presenting as heterosexual) is illustrative (see King, 2004). More nuanced discussions use the phrases *MSM* (men who have sex with men) and *WSW* (women who have sex with women) to describe sexual behavior, but self-identity in this typology remains unquestioned.

Gender identity is about personal feelings regarding one's sense of self about being a man or a woman (maleness and femaleness), apart from one's body parts. How a person presents these feelings to the world is considered her or his *gender expression*. These terms open the discussion to the topics of *transgender* and *transsexuality*. *Transgender* is a term that describes gender identity. People may have an identity—that is, man, woman, or both, or neither—that does not correspond to their actual genetic makeup and anatomy. *Transsexuality* is a state of being transgender but taking action to affirm the felt self-identity. Both transgender and transsexual people present unique circumstances, far beyond the question of which lavatory to use, that must be navigated in organizational environments.

In organizational settings, we find people in same-gender relationships who self-identify as straight; individuals who, while biologically appearing as male, self-identify as female (and vice versa); and individuals who consider themselves both or neither. All of this may result in considerable confusion, denial, fear, uncertainty, and discord in organizations. Heterosexism and homophobia may reflect this dissonance.

Heterosexism can be described as the attitude that all people are, or should be, heterosexual. It often is "an ideological system that denies, denigrates, and stigmatizes any non-heterosexual form of behaviour, relationship, or community" (Herek, 1990, p. 316). *Homophobia*, the affective, irrational dislike of lesbians and gay men, has become a contested word, especially with the rise of the religious right in the United States. Once labeled as homophobic for their antigay, antilesbian sentiments, this group, having gained considerable public currency, openly rejects this marker. They perceive their negative attitudes toward sexual orientation as entirely rational and justifiable (Linneman, 2004). Herek (2004) advances the notion that a new vocabulary is needed and offers *sexual prejudice* (p. 6). Additional terms that have been suggested as replacements for the word *homophobia* include *homo-hatred, homo-aversion,* and *homo-negativity.* They are employed in these pages.

Intersexuals (people with a combination of male and female biology and physiology, sometimes incorrectly lumped together as hermaphrodites) are not directly addressed in this volume but should be at least mentioned here. Fausto-Sterling (2005) offers that intersex conditions (note the plural, "conditions") contribute to "challenging ideas about the male/female divide" (p. 116). The discourse constructed by people with intersex conditions is that the social problem associated with them is not gender related, but rather is stigma and trauma from society. No research studies on the intersection of intersexual issues and organizations, or the workplace, were found in a literature review for this volume. Informal and narrative presentations of the topic appear on the Internet and include "intersexual coming out" in the workplace and loss of employment after self-disclosure. (Readers are referred to the Intersex Society of North America for information on intersexual persons; http://www.isna.org/.)

Of course, the use of the term *queer* must be addressed head-on. It elicits passionate responses in many people. *Queer* is used in at least two distinct ways. One is as a means to avoid the cumbersome acronym LGBT, that is, as an umbrella term for the collection of sexual minorities. This usage of the word has value, including establishing an identifiable "we" (or "them") that generates political and personal identity. Another use of *queer* suggests that identities are always multiple, fluid, mobile, contingent, unstable (labile), and fragmented. It challenges fixed, sedimented notions such as gay, lesbian, and straight. *Queer* in this formation "attempts to transform an epithet into a label of pride and militance [sic]. . . . Use of the word is . . . debated within the gay community. Some argue that it reflects the internalization of homophobic attitudes, while others argue that it signifies defiance of straight culture" (Rosenblum and Travis, 2003, p. 7). Even more vexing is the notion that *queer* must not be understood by the question, "What is it?" but rather by the interrogative, "How does it function?" An answer to the latter is that *queer* destabilizes and contests the meaning of "normal." This raises the possibility that there are straight queers too.

In this volume, readers will note the use of the term *sexual minority,* which is to some a problematic formation for at least two reasons. There is a debate, not engaged here, regarding whether LGBTQ people should be labeled with the term *sexual* since so much of our lives is not about sexuality. In addition, the use of *minority* implies a civil rights script, and the comparison of "gay rights" to "civil rights," especially in the context of African American struggles, remains contentious (Gates, 1999). Without engaging in these debates, the term *sexual minority* is employed here since it illustrates that a subset of the population experiences pervasive prejudice, social oppression, and discrimination based on sexual orientation or gender expression (Chung, 2001).

A Critique

A valid criticism of the volume will be the partial (although by no means absent) coverage of intersectionality. Identity markers such as class, ability, ethnicity, and race overlap with sexual orientation and gender identity; that is, many people have multiple minority status. What it is like to be a gay, disabled, labor-class woman of color, for example, can only be conjectured. An exception includes the intersection of gender with sexual minority status, which is presented through specific coverage of lesbian issues.

Intersections from specific contexts could have been incorporated, but space disallowed it. Contemporary instances include LGBTQ issues and immigration and occupational settings; sports organizations; the military-industrial complex; sex worker industries; political organizations; religious organizations; legal and medical organizations; international organizations; and many more.

Another critique lies in the incomplete inclusion of bisexuals and gender-variant people—the BTQ in LGBTQ. Perhaps to some, the umbrella acronym LGBTQ will seem to be overused. Rarely do other sexualities get elaborated, such as *two-spirited* (a term employed by Native Americans and First Nation peoples, denoting that both masculine and feminine spirits live within some individuals, constituting a "third-gender" category), acknowledged in Chapter Five). We hope that readers will piece together the notion that there are more than two genders (the socially defined sex roles, values, and beliefs related to the state of being male or female) . . . , more than two gender expressions (what we do to communicate how we feel as male or female) . . . , and more than two sexual orientations (gay and straight). In fact, I hope that this volume challenges readers to question all of the binaries that dominate and commandeer most of our lives. Doing so will open up new space for unheralded voices in arenas well beyond sexual minorities in organizational settings and perhaps will be the harbinger of a new social revolution.

Robert J. Hill
Editor

References

Chung, Y. B. "Work Discrimination and Coping Strategies: Conceptual Frameworks for Counseling Lesbian, Gay, and Bisexual Clients." *Career Development Quarterly,* 2001, *50,* 33–44.

Fausto-Sterling, A. "Two Sexes Are Not Enough." In R. Fiske-Rusciano and V. Cyrus (eds.), *Experiencing Race, Class, and Gender in the United States.* (4th ed.) New York: McGraw-Hill, 2005.

Gates, H. L., Jr. "Backlash?" In L. Gross and J. D. Woods (eds.), *The Columbia Reader on Lesbian and Gay Men in Media, Society, and Politics.* New York: Columbia University Press, 1999.

Herek, G. M. "The Context of Anti-Gay Violence." *Journal of Interpersonal Violence,* 1990, *5,* 316–333.

Herek, G. M. "Beyond 'Homophobia': Thinking About Sexual Prejudice and Stigma in the Twenty-First Century." *Sexuality Research and Social Policy,* 2004, *1*(2), 6–24.

Hostetler, A. J., and Herdt, G. H. "Culture, Sexual Lifeways, and Developmental Subjectivities: Rethinking Sexual Taxonomies." *Social Research,* 1998, *65*(2), 249–291.

King, J. L. *On the Down Low: A Journey into the Lives of "Straight" Black Men Who Sleep with Men.* New York: Random House, 2004.

Lather, P. "Troubling Clarity: The Politics of Accessible Language." *Harvard Educational Review,* 1996, *66*(3), 525–545.

Linneman, T. J. "Homophobia and Hostility: Christian Conservative Reactions to the Political and Cultural Progress of Lesbians and Gay Men." *Sexuality Research and Social Policy,* 2004, *1*(2), 56–76.

Mezirow, J. *Transformative Dimensions of Adult Learning.* San Francisco: Jossey-Bass, 1991.

Ragins, B. R. "Sexual Orientation in the Workplace: The Unique Work and Career Experiences of Gay, Lesbian and Bisexual Workers." *Research in Personnel and Human Resources Management,* 2004, *23,* 35–120.

Rosenblum, K. E., and Travis, T.-M. C. *The Meaning of Difference: American Constructions of Race, Sex and Gender, Social Class, and Sexual Orientation.* New York: McGraw-Hill, 2003.

ROBERT J. HILL *is associate professor of adult education in the Department of Lifelong Education, Administration, and Policy at the University of Georgia, Athens.*

1

This chapter looks at what it is like to be queer in organizations, with an emphasis on adult and continuing education providers.

What's It Like to Be Queer Here?

Robert J. Hill

The line, "Ours is an organizational society," opens the book *Organizations: Rational, Natural, and Open Systems,* by Scott (2003), who goes on to say, "Organizations are a prominent, if not the dominant, characteristic of modern society" (p. 3). They are complex structures that carry out a variety of tasks and processes to meet their vision, mission, and value statements. No single definition can capture this complexity, in part due to the bewildering range of organizations that exist. This chapter, as does this volume as a whole, reflects the reality of a variety of organizations, with a focus on adult, continuing, and higher education providers.

Hatch (1997) offers that organizations "are usefully conceptualized as technologies, social structures, cultures, and physical structures that overlay and interpenetrate one another within the context of an environment" (p. 15). They help "achieve goals beyond the reach of the individual" (Scott, 2003, p. 3). Missing in most organizational formulations is the notion that organizations are places where human sexuality also intersects with technologies, culture, and society. They are spaces where the politics of identity and sexuality are played out. Like so many other social institutions, educational settings across the life span are caught in the cultural war of values currently raging in the United States and elsewhere (Wilson, 1999) regarding human sexuality. This chapter explores several arenas in the debate around sexual orientation and gender identity in organizations.

Adult, continuing, and higher education are sites of both tolerance and homo- and transphobia. They are no exceptions to socially entrenched heteronormativity. The fight to crack open these terrains has proven to be a challenging task requiring the courage and persistence of queer educators,

NEW DIRECTIONS FOR ADULT AND CONTINUING EDUCATION, no. 112, Winter 2006 © 2006 Wiley Periodicals, Inc.
Published online in Wiley InterScience (www.interscience.wiley.com) • DOI: 10.1002/ace.232

graduate students, and our allies (Grace and Hill, 2004). Until 1993, lesbian, gay, bisexual, transgender, and queer (LGBTQ) concerns were not addressed by educators in adult and continuing education (Hill, 2003b). In the ensuing years, this has changed significantly. Hill (2003b) cites three moments that have been pivotal in bringing queer vision and voice to adult education. The first moment was the formation of the Lesbian, Gay, Bisexual, Transgender, Queer & Allies Caucus (LGBTQ & AC) at the Thirty-Fourth Adult Education Research Conference (AERC), Pennsylvania State University, in 1993 (initiated by me and Libby Tisdell, coauthor of Chapter Six). The founding of the caucus constituted the first formal queer (and friends) network in the field. The second moment was the earliest LGBTQ-themed presentation at the AERC, University of Tennessee, Knoxville, in 1994 (Hill, 1995). The third moment was the inaugural LGBTQ & AC AERC Pre-Conference in San Francisco in 2003, which has continued to explore fugitive forms of social knowledge. Fugitive knowledge is that knowledge that is constructed by individuals and groups outside of officially recognized knowledge-makers or canonists of a field. It is knowledge that has not been censored or reformulated to fit existing and often hegemonic meanings. The pre-conference remains a vital dialogical space to explore what counts as knowledge and what knowledge counts in adult and continuing education (Grace and Hill, 2004). These three events have catalyzed hopes and aspirations within organizations in these fields (Hill, 2003b).

Organizations: Shaped by the Wider Social Milieu

While organizations on the landscape react and respond to the environment differently, the challenge of dealing with sexual minorities, that is, LGBTQ people, in organizational settings is formidable. LGBTQ individuals have traditionally joined organizations where the dominant organizational culture has been silence regarding sexual orientation and gender identity, with the concomitant expectation of invisibility, to which sexual minorities have often complied.

Sexual minorities "constitute one of the largest, but least studied, minority groups in the workforce" (Ragins, 2004, p. 35), including in education. In recent years, adapting to changes in society, "corporate America has moved rapidly . . . toward recognizing and correcting some of the imbalances long prevalent in [the arena of sexual minority workplace rights]" (Mills and Herrschaft, 1999, p. 5). For example, in 2005, 5.6 million people worked at companies that attained perfect scores (100 percent) on the Human Rights Campaign Corporate Equality Index (Human Rights Campaign Foundation, 2005) for LGBT-fair workplace policies and practices. And 113 companies had progressive transgender nondiscrimination protection, up 92 percent from the previous year. Although limited data exist, it appears that within formal and nonformal adult education venues, the change has been less sweeping. The experiences of LGBTQ staff and faculty in K–12 settings and adult, continuing, and higher education have been explored in only limited ways (see, for example, Allen, 1995; Friskopp, 1995; Griffin, 1992; Harbeck, 1997; Mintz and Rothblum, 1997; Niesche, 2003; Ristock, 1998; Ropers-Huilman, 1999; Tisdell and Taylor, 1999; Wall and Evans, 2000; and new publications such as the *Journal of Gay and Lesbian Issues in Education*).

A Growing Diversified Landscape

Hatch (1997) argues that "one of the most promising sources of [organizational] innovation. . . . predicted for the future is the growing diversity" (p. 319). Larkey (1996) provides references to a host of benefits that arise from the increasing diversity found in workplaces, including the impact of human variety on organizational productivity and effectiveness, its impact on the bottom line (through members' individual contributions and through the impacts of diverse populations working cooperatively), and diversity's influence on creativity and the quality of ideas. The last point is especially significant for educational settings. It is salient to note that the value of diversity to virtually all organizations was originally conceived without reference to sexual orientation, gender identity, or gender expression; it stopped at race, gender, national origin, and ethnicity. For instance, in discussions of diversity in vocational and career topics, in the turn toward sexual minorities, it was "only in the 1980s and 1990s [that] any substantial amount of literature emerge[d]" (Croteau, 1996, p. 195). Even then, most organizations explored diversity from the perspective of sexual orientation (the object of one's physical and emotional desires stemming from cultural, economic, political, and historical contexts) and omitted two additional components necessary for a successful diversity equation: gender identity (the personal awareness of the self as male/man, female/woman, both or neither), and gender expression (the outward display of a person's self-awareness of gender).

Organizations: Shaping the Wider Social Milieu

Not only are organizations influenced by society and culture, but the wider milieu is shaped in part by organizations. That is, organizations help to create social change, wittingly or unwittingly. This is done by actions taken (Scott, 2003) and influences exerted in both the public and private spheres. In fact, some authors consider organizations as "the new frontier for lesbian, gay and bisexual rights" (Raeburn, 2004, p. 1) in the larger social context.

Organizational learning regarding LGBTQ issues, through education, training, mentoring, associating with sexual minorities, and other venues, can be transformative to the individual, with subsequent impacts on society outside the organization. Carl Rogers proposed that *significant learning* is "learning which makes a difference—in [an] individual's behavior, in the course of action [chosen] . . . in attitudes and in personality" (1961, p. 280).

To be sure, the effects of this significant learning do not cease when an employee punches the time clock to go home or drives out of the school parking lot.

Some authors have argued that LGBTQ workplace advocacy and activism constitute a new social movement (Raeburn, 2004). This queer workplace movement, related to sexual minority rights, displays characteristics attributed to other new social movements (for example, the women's movement and the environmental movement), such as being a site of learning, meaning making, and resistance (Finger, 1989; Habermas, 1981; Welton, 1993).

Affirming Organizational Practices: Dismantling the Lavender Ceiling

In recent years, an LGBTQ-rights workplace movement to support sexual minorities in organizational settings has taken hold. This movement has been shaped by and is shaping organizations' cultural contexts. For instance, the Board of the Society for Human Resource Management has approved a resolution to include sexual orientation in its diversity statement (Day and Schoenrade, 1997). Nevertheless, widespread heterosexism flourishes, and sexual minorities still fear discrimination in the workplace (Day and Schoenrade, 1997). The *lavender ceiling,* a term used to "describe the kinds of systemic barriers which prevent recruitment, retention, and promotion of openly gay and lesbian people" (Swan, 1995, p. 51), is often an invariable threat. Systemic barriers manifest in several ways, especially through systemic exclusion of sexual minorities and systemic inclusion of straight discourses (Wade, 1995). Systemic exclusion is the absence of affirming policies, rules, role models, mentors, internship programs, recruitment, advancement to highly visible positions, messages, merited awards, and images about LGBTQ members. Systemic inclusion of only heterosexuals is the "process of institutionalized heterosexism" (Wade, 1995, p. 45). In higher education, the lavender ceiling may be encountered during the tenure process (McDonough, 2002).

Diversity Training, Education, and Skills Development

Educational efforts in organizations should include prejudice-reduction strategies related to sexual orientation, gender identity, and gender expression within diversity models. Palmer (1989) has developed a three-part typology of diversity paradigms. One paradigm, termed "the golden rule," describes diversity as a moral issue and inclusion as the right thing to do. Another paradigm is the "righting the wrong" model, which seeks to redress the wrongs of exclusion. The third paradigm, "valuing diversity," includes the strategy of valuing difference for the contributions it makes to an organization and the increasing diversity awareness and cultural competency in members. In the third model, the key is "not necessarily to change people, but to change the organizational systems and culture so that the organization can become inclusive" (Esty, Griffin, and Hirsch, 1995, p. 2). It is within the third model that learning organizations (Senge, 1990) will have the greatest impacts on LGBTQ members' lives. Learning organizations, with their collection of individuals who constantly develop the means to explore the big picture and understand the relationships among its parts, can be ideal for promoting an inclusive culture. Sustained diversity training and education programs (continuous contact with LGBTQ content) in organizational settings are crucial to this.

Hill (2003a) has recommended actions appropriate for adult, continuing, and higher education organizations, in the following categories (selected from Hill, 2003a):

- *Cultural competency of members.* Develop and implement plans for cultural competence in order to educate employees, students, faculty, administrators, and counselors on LBGTQ issues, learning inclusive language, confronting language and behaviors that marginalize LGBTQ people, recognizing antigay bias and violence, directing organizational publications to provide adequate and fair coverage of LGBTQ events and issues, and recognizing that diversity exists within diversity (LGBTQ identity and behavior cross racial, ethnic, ability, and age lines).
- *Structural amendments.* Organizational leadership's implementation of an LGBTQ-inclusive diversity strategy (including nondiscrimination policies for LGBTQ people); development (or enlargement) of reference information and media resources on LGBTQ issues.
- *Behavioral protection.* Apply disciplinary measures to those found violating policies related to sexual orientation, gender identity, or gender expression; train organization members to initiate investigative procedures in the event of infractions; and train administrators to enforce LGBTQ-protective policies.
- *Administrative affairs.* Fully implement, publish, and enforce antidiscrimination policies with LGBTQ protection; include LGBTQ people in diversity and multicultural initiatives; broaden the scope of the term *minority* to include LGBTQ members; show how LGBTQ employees' experiences can be qualitatively different from those of other minorities as they steer through organizational cultures.
- *Counseling services and appropriate health care.* Include assistance to cope with stress from society and organizational culture that often marginalizes or oppresses LGBTQ individuals; health education that includes specific and forthright information appropriate to LGBTQ communities, especially on the unique health concerns of lesbians.
- *Engagement.* Connect organizational efforts to those outside the organization; in higher education, coach preservice teachers in college courses about LGBTQ issues, and offer in-service training in partnership with pub-

lic and private schools; establish a liaison between the organization's LGBTQ membership and the local community.

Organizational education is a process (Winfeld, 2005). It should be both open-ended and open-minded. To be effective, it must be sustained over the long haul rather than an infrequent event.

Gender-Variant Support: Unique Situations

Gender variations are replete in occupational settings. For instance, it is esti- mated that more than 200,000 people have transitioned in the United States from the sex of their birth since the 1950s (Winfeld, 2005). Transitioning employees are those "who are moving outside the socially accepted stan- dards of dress, physiology and/or behavior of their birth gender—often . . . challenging community standards about what is gender-appropriate self- identification, appearance or expression" (Human Rights Campaign Foun- dation, 2006). Organizations present transsexuals with unique challenges and situations. In most places, there is scant legal protection for workplace gender nonconformity. In order to shield all parties in an organization, pro- tection based on gender identity or gender expression should be included in nondiscrimination and antiharassment policies and incorporated in the organization's sustained diversity education programs. Winfeld (2005) reports that "whatever a workplace education program imparts about [trans- sexuals] is going to represent a 100 percent increase in the knowledge and understanding of the average person" (p. 86).

Without written protection, it is very common for transsexuals to be fired from their jobs or to experience harassment and violence in organiza- tional settings. (For the story of one transsexual academic, see McCloskey, 1999.) Walworth (1998) reports anecdotally that transsexuals desiring to transition physically are "strongly motivated to earn enough money to pay for the desired procedures and to maintain above-average performance in order to keep their jobs" (p. 54). She also notes that once transition is com- pleted, the employee is likely to be productive due to greater self-esteem.

Awkward situations may arise with transitioning employees who inter- face with the general public. Policies to establish boundaries should be announced before an employee makes public her or his decision to transi- tion. Sustained diversity training programs that already deal with gender identity and gender expression reduce the intensity of reaction to the announcement. The bottom line is for organizations to show their commit- ment to safe, nondiscriminatory environments for transemployees.

Acceptance of . . . and Backlash to Diversity Change

Bumiller (2005) notes that "the cultural change [regarding "gay" issues] has been swift, radical, and seemingly irreversible" (p. 117). This sea change has

New Directions for Adult and Continuing Education • DOI: 10.1002/ace

had positive and negative outcomes for LGBTQ people in organizations, including those related to adult and continuing education. The Henry J. Kaiser Family Foundation (2001) reported that most (76 percent of the 405 sexual minorities surveyed) lesbians, gay men, and bisexuals believe there is greater acceptance of them, but 74 percent also reported fear, discrimination, and violence. One of every three (32 percent) reported being a target of physical hostility because of their sexual orientation. In a companion survey of 2,283 adults among the general (nongay) public conducted by the foundation, similar views were noted: 78 percent believed that gay men and lesbians experience at least some prejudice and discrimination, including more than half (57 percent) who thought the discrimination was "a lot" and 39 percent who believed there is more violence toward gays and lesbians in the United States today than just a few years ago.

Backlash to queer presence is one of the consequences of gay-affirming changes in society (and in organizations). Backlash takes many forms. In organizations with active diversity programs that include antioppression education and training, resistance is one of the responses (Kumashiro, 2002). In adult education, Hill (2003b) found that early in the development of the AERC LGBTQ & Allies Caucus, resistance took the form of neutralization, denial, and avoidance by some AERC attendees and organizers. Backlash assumed the form of subtle policing of the AERC borders by certain resistant educators; fortunately, this did not represent the majority of experiences. Within AERC in the main, sexual minorities, especially lesbian and gay members, have been affirmed, enabled, and supported. Yet when policing occurs, it cannot be ignored since it represents marginalization and the silencing of vital voices.

In organizations, backlash may emerge when straight members demand "equal time" based on objections to "homosexuality," often due to personal or religious reasons. This is not uncommon in the growing climate of right-wing fundamentalist and the religious-based politics of intolerance in the United States (see Fisher and others, 1994). Backlash also emerges in the form of antigay shareholder activism (Raeburn, 2004) at corporate stockholder meetings. A counterpart to this is the resistance of some college and university boards of regents to sexual minority rights on campuses.

Backlash to supportive policies and practices toward LGBTQ people can be overcome. Thomas (2005, citing Cox and Beale, 1997) suggests that how an organization conveys its "gay-friendly" message is critical (see Chapter Eight, this volume). Support should be couched within the overall educational commitment to equal opportunity. Training should uncouple a person's sexual orientation (or gender identity) from the principle of equal opportunity for all qualified people. Organizations should "provide . . . the opportunity [for people to] select themselves out of positions in which they feel that they will have to compromise their religious beliefs or moral sentiments" (Thomas, 2005, p. 116).

Conclusion

Organizational and occupational settings are never divorced from the dynamics of oppression and marginalization. Hostile environments for sexual minorities result in conflict, lack of organizational commitment, likelihood of job turnover, less career satisfaction, poor job attitudes, and stress (Ragins, 2004; Thomas, 2005).

It is through affirming policies, practices, and cultures that a salubrious climate is created for LGBTQ people in organizations. Climate is critical to answering the question, "What's it like to be queer here?" In organizations where the climate enforces silence and invisibility, professional and personal energy is drained (Spradlin, 1998). Passing, that is, concealing information about the self, exacts a toll on both individuals and organizations. For sexual minority members, being out, while having potential for backlash from exposure, can be a significant factor in generating an encouraging environment since, as Horvath and Ryan (2003) have shown, previous contact with lesbian, gay, or bisexual people is a significant predictor of supportive attitudes by nongays.

There are "radically different ways of imagining sex and gender arrangements and identities" (Altman, 2004, p. 63). Organizations will never be able to individually address all of these ways; however, they can create climates, through training and education, policy formulation and implementation, and leadership, where employees of all identities can say, "It's great to be queer here!" Organizations and the societies that depend on them will reap immense benefits.

References

Allen, K. "Opening the Classroom Closet: Sexual Orientation and Self-Disclosure." *Family Relations*, 1995, *44*, 136–141.

Altman, D. "Sexuality and Globalization." *Sexuality Research and Social Policy*, 2004, *1*(1), 63–68.

Bumiller, E. "Cold Feet: Why America Has Gay Marriage Jitters." In R. Fiske-Rusciano and V. Cyrus (eds.), *Experiencing Race, Class, and Gender in the United States*. (4th ed.) New York: McGraw-Hill, 2005.

Croteau, J. M. "Research on the Work Experiences of Lesbian, Gay, and Bisexual People: An Integrative Review of Methodology and Findings." *Journal of Vocational Behavior*, 1996, *48*, 195–209.

Day, N. E., and Schoenrade, P. "Staying in the Closet Versus Coming Out: Relationships Between Communication About Sexual Orientation and Work Attitudes." *Personnel Psychology*, 1997, *50*, 147–163.

Esty, K., Griffin, R., and Hirsch, M. S. *Workplace Diversity*. Avon, Mass.: Adams Media Corporation, 1995.

Finger, M. "New Social Movements and Their Implications for Adult Education." *Adult Education Quarterly*, 1989, *40*(1), 15–21.

Fisher, R. D., and others. "Religiousness, Religious Orientation, and Attitudes Towards Gays and Lesbians." *Journal of Applied Social Psychology*, 1994, *24*, 614–630.

Friskopp, A. *Straight Jobs, Gay Lives: Gay and Lesbian Professionals, the Harvard Business School, and the American Workplace*. New York: Scribner, 1995.

Grace, A., and Hill, R. J. "Positioning Queer in Adult Education: Intervening in Politics and Praxis." *Studies in the Education of Adults,* 2004, *36*(2), 167–189.

Griffin, P. "From Hiding Out to Coming Out: Empowering Lesbian and Gay Educators." In K. M. Harbeck (ed.), *Coming Out of the Classroom Closet.* Binghamton, N.Y.: Harrington Park Press, 1992.

Habermas, J. "New Social Movements." *Telos,* 1981, *49,* 33–37.

Harbeck, K. M. (ed.). *Gay and Lesbian Educators: Personal Freedoms, Public Constraints.* Boston: Amethyst Press and Productions, 1997.

Hatch, M. J. *Organization Theory: Modern, Symbolic, and Postmodern Perspectives.* New York: Oxford University Press, 1997.

Henry J. Kaiser Family Foundation. "Inside-OUT: A Report on the Experiences of Lesbians, Gays and Bisexuals in America and the Public's Views on Issues and Policies Related to Sexual Orientation." Menlo Park, Calif.: Kaiser Foundation, 2001. http://www.kff.org/kaiserpolls/upload/New-Surveys-on-Experiences-of-Lesbians-Gays-and-Bisexuals-and-the-Public-s-Views-Related-to-Sexual-Orientation-Chart-Pack.pdf. Accessed Feb. 16, 2006.

Hill, R. J. "A Critique of Heterocentric Discourse in Adult Education: A Critical Review." *Adult Education Quarterly,* 1995, *45*(3), 142–158.

Hill, R. J. "Pressing Policy Issues: Safe and Supportive Opportunities for Lesbian, Gay, Bisexual, Transgender, and Queer Learners in Higher Education." Paper presented at the Forty-Fourth Annual Adult Education Research Conference, San Francisco State University, San Francisco, June 2003a.

Hill, R. J. "Working Memory at AERC: A Queer Welcome . . . and a Retrospective." Proceedings of the First LGBTQ Pre-Conference at the Forty-Fourth Annual Adult Education Research Conference, San Francisco State University, San Francisco, 2003b.

Horvath, M., and Ryan. A. "Antecedents and Potential Moderators of the Relationship Between Attitudes and Hiring Discrimination on the Basis of Sexual Orientation." *Sex Roles,* 2003, *48,* 115–130.

Human Rights Campaign Foundation. *Corporate Equality Index: A Report Card on Gay, Lesbian, Bisexual, Transgender Equality in Corporate America.* 2005. http://www.hrc.org/Template.cfm?Section=Corporate_Equality_Index&Template=/ContentManagement/ContentDisplay.cfm&ContentID=28841. Accessed Mar. 17, 2006.

Human Rights Campaign Foundation. *Worker Gender Transition Guidelines for Transgender Employees, Managers, and Human Resource Professionals.* 2006. http://www.hrc.org/Content/NavigationMenu/Work_Life/Get_Informed2/Transgender_Issues/WorkplaceGenderTransitionGuidelines-May2006.pdf. Accessed Apr. 28, 2006.

Kumashiro, K. K. "'Posts' Perspectives on Anti-Oppression Education in Social Studies, English, Mathematics, and Science Classrooms." *Educational Researcher,* 2002, *30*(3), 3–12.

Larkey, L. K. "Toward a Theory of Communicative Interactions in Culturally Diverse Workgroups." *Academy of Management Review,* 1996, *21*(2), 463–492.

McCloskey, D. N. *Crossing: A Memoir.* Chicago: University of Chicago Press, 1999.

McDonough, P. M. "Resisting Common Injustice: Tenure Politics, Department Politics, Gay and Lesbian Politics." In J. E. Cooper and D. D. Stevens (eds.), *Tenure in the Sacred Grove: Issues and Strategies for Women and Minority Faculty.* Albany: State University of New York Press, 2002.

Mills, K. I., and Herrschaft, D. *The State of the Workplace for Lesbian, Gay, Bisexual and Transgendered Americans.* Washington, D.C.: Human Rights Campaign, 1999.

Mintz, B., and Rothblum, E. (eds.). *Lesbians in Academia: Degrees of Freedom.* New York: Routledge, 1997.

Niesche, R. "Power and Homosexuality in the Teaching Workplace." *Social Alternatives,* 2003, *22*(2), 43–47.

Palmer, J. D. "Three Paradigms for Diversity Change Leaders." *Organization Development Practitioner,* 1989, *21*(1), 15–18.

Raeburn, N. C. *Changing Corporate America from Inside Out: Lesbian and Gay Workplace Rights.* Minneapolis: University of Minnesota Press, 2004.

Ragins, B. R. "Sexual Orientation in the Workplace: The Unique Work and Career Experiences of Gay, Lesbian and Bisexual Workers." *Research in Personnel and Human Resources Management,* 2004, *23,* 35–120.

Ristock, J. *Inside the Academy and Out: Lesbian/Gay Queer Studies and Social Action.* Toronto: University of Toronto Press, 1998.

Rogers, C. *On Becoming a Person.* Boston: Houghton Mifflin, 1961.

Ropers-Huilman, B. "Social Justice in the Classroom: Understanding the Implications of Interlocking Oppressions." *College Teaching,* 1999, 47(3), 91–95.

Scott, W. R. *Organizations: Rational, Natural, and Open Systems.* Upper Saddle River, N.J.: Prentice Hall, 2003.

Senge, P. M. *The Fifth Discipline. The Art and Practice of the Learning Organization.* New York: Random House, 1990.

Spradlin, A. L. "The Price of 'Passing': A Lesbian Perspective on Authenticity in Organizations." *Management Communication Quarterly,* 1998, 11(4), 598–605. (ERIC 563 767)

Swan, W. "The Lavender Ceiling: How It Works in Practice." In W. Swan (ed.), *Breaking the Silence: Gay, Lesbian and Bisexual Issues in Public Administration.* Washington, D.C.: American Society for Public Administration, 1995.

Thomas, K. M. *Diversity Dynamics in the Workplace.* Belmont, Calif.: Wadsworth, 2005.

Tisdell, E., and Taylor, E. "Out of the Closet: Lesbian and Gay Adult Educators and Sexual Orientation Issues in the University Learning Environment." In *Proceedings of the Thirty-Sixth Annual Adult Education Research Conference.* University of Alberta, Edmonton, Alberta, Canada, 1999.

Wade, S. K. "Values and Norms: Gays, Lesbians and Bisexuals in the Public Sector Workplace." In W. Swan (ed.), *Breaking the Silence: Gay, Lesbian and Bisexual Issues in Public Administration.* Washington, D.C.: American Society for Public Administration, 1995.

Wall, V. A., and Evans, N. J. *Toward Acceptance: Sexual Orientation Issues on Campus.* Lanham, Md.: University Press of America, 2000.

Walworth, J. *Transsexual Workers: An Employer's Guide.* Los Angeles: Center for Gender Sanity, 1998.

Welton, M. "Social Revolutionary Learning: The New Social Movements as Learning Sites." *Adult Education Quarterly,* 1993, 43(3), 152–164.

Wilson, B. P. "The Culture Wars in Higher Education." *Phi Kappa Phi Journal,* Winter 1999, 14–18.

Winfeld, L. *Straight Talk About Gays in the Workplace: Creating an Inclusive, Productive Environment for Everyone in Your Organization.* Binghampton, N.Y.: Haworth Press, 2005.

ROBERT J. HILL *is associate professor of adult education in the Department of Lifelong Education, Administration, and Policy at the University of Georgia, Athens.*

2

This chapter provides a framework to facilitate self-awareness, self-knowledge, diversity training, and cultural awareness and appreciation for all adults, based on understanding the development of sexual identity and workplace issues for LGBTQ adults.

A Transformative Learning Perspective of Continuing Sexual Identity Development in the Workplace

Kathleen P. King, Susan C. Biro

With weekly headlines vacillating between "San Francisco Weds Gay Couples" (2004), "Court Annuls San Francisco Gay Marriages" (2004), and "Neighbors Denounce Anti-gay Hate Crime" (2005), and prosecution of sexual harassment in the U.S. Supreme Court, mandated diversity training, and widely tolerated hate talk, it is no surprise that adults, both straight and not, hardly stand a chance of knowing which way the winds blow at any given time.

However, in the midst of this rapidly changing current of popular and legal opinion, heterosexuality remains the dominant model of sexual orientation and identity. Therefore, lesbian, gay, bisexual, transgender, and queer (LGBTQ) individuals face constant challenges to their self-identity through the media, public interactions, personal relationships, community, family rituals, legal transactions and rights, and the workplace. Wherever LGBTQ adults go or look in the mainstream, they are swimming upstream, against the current. They are a pink salmon in a school of spotted salmon, as it were. They are constantly reminded, "You are not one of us."

The Need

In the midst of the abounding contradictions of public opinion and behavior, LGBTQ adults have a pressing need not only to discover successful ways to cope with their world but also a personal resolution within them-

selves. Indeed, if this personal resolution has not been achieved, the need to find it can be quite urgent. In many models of sexual identity development, the perspective is that this development is linear and terminal. Instead, transformative learning offers a framework of a continuing personal journey of sexual identity development. This framework is a more fluid, evolving development, which is essential given that the context, environment, and social, political, religious, and cultural values and opinions concerning LGBTQ issues are also contradictory, inflammatory, and constantly changing.

In the specific context of professional life, there are many issues surrounding LGBTQ adults. For instance, consider how adults cope with the following: politically acceptable lifestyles versus their own, an undisclosed versus publicly stated self, keeping religion and politics separate from the workplace, dealing with moralized codes of behavior, and instances and consequences of hidden privilege. Complicating the situation for adult workers is the fact that each of these issues is amplified by multiple shades of variation.

At the very least, we are faced with a few fundamental questions for the workplace: Is there a framework that can help us understand how LGBTQ adults cope and reconcile the personal journey with the professional workplace? How can we use this framework to help LGBTQ adults successfully cope in the workplace? How can we use this framework to help inform straight adults about their LGBTQ coworkers and thus possibly better understand this additional layer of complexity in the workplace?

Wishik and Pierce Model

In 1991, Wishik and Pierce proposed a model that traces and examines the "dominant" and "subordinate" pathways of mainstream and LGBTQ sexual orientations and sexual identities. In a heterosexual-dominated society, sexual identity is ascribed to individuals based on gender.

Wishik and Pierce (1991) recognized sexual identity as having a fluid nature in which some adults move from one identity to another, or more, over time. Their model has two major streams along which adults may originally identify: (1) the dominant heterosexuality (heterosexual) and (2) the subordinate (lesbian and gay). There are also middle streams of bisexual or transgender identity development that can emerge from each of the other two. Rising and falling waves of questions and experience progress along these pathways, exerting pressure and creating a need to cope with an individual's social and personal identities (Cass, 1984; Taylor, 1999).

In Wishik and Pierce's model, these pathways are uniquely traced through personal questioning, learning of diverse cultures and perspectives, critical questioning, and new experiences, personal concepts, and personal relationships to embrace diversity in sexuality.

Transformative Learning

The theory of transformative learning originally focused on the cognitive process that adults experience as they examine values, beliefs, and assumptions that they may not have previously considered. It addresses the possible significant shift in adults' understanding of their meaning perspective (Mezirow, 1978; Mezirow and Associates, 1990), otherwise known as their frame of reference (Cranton, 1994; Mezirow and Associates, 2000). Transformative learning may start with a "disorienting dilemma" and progress through a dynamic pathway of stages, including personal questioning, deliberation, reexamination, new perspectives, trial stages, and final reintegration of a new frame of reference for understanding their world. Mezirow's original theory has been challenged from many perspectives, and the adult learning field has recognized that it needs to account for other dimensions, including emotions, nonlinear development, spiritual aspects, social action, and cultural interpretations (King, 2005).

However, the LGBTQ community recognized that transformative learning had helpful parallels in LGBT sexual identity development. Brooks and Edwards (1997) and then Donnelly (2001) especially examined the transformative learning experience of lesbian women coming out. In 2003, King provided a working model for dialogue and understanding of these LGBTQ adult learning experiences. Bridging transformative learning and Wishik and Pierce's model (1991) offer a basis for adults to reflect on their experiences using adult learning and a heuristic, self-understanding framework. Such a perspective emphasizes that as critical questioning, understanding, and construction continue, these inward changes result in decision for action. Therefore, adults experience "changing from the inside out" (King, 2003, p. 65). Through critical reflection, learning, and action, adults can move through complex and multidimensional stages of understanding in discovering or creating their sexual identities.

This approach is not intended to categorize adults' sexual identity in predetermined definitions and requisites. The ultimate goal is to be able to value and embrace multiple interpretations of sexual identity across individuals. In addition, it is recognized and appreciated that bisexual and transgendered (BT) adults may have more complex journeys to work through in their experience and in their relationships. Bisexual and transgendered adults face the challenges and oppression of dealing with a heteronormative society; in addition, they may face resistance or rejection from some members of the gay and lesbian community as well. In order to be inclusive and recognize the similarities of experiences, all LGBTQ adults are addressed with the conceptualization of this model, but at the same time, BTQ adults may find further adaptation of this model warranted at this point.

Table 2.1. LGBTQ TL Process Integrated with Other Models

LGBTQ TL Process (King, 2003)	Wishik and Pierce Model (1991)	Mezirow Model (1991)
	Opposition	
Question	Encounter new views	1. A disorienting dilemma
Risk	Question	2. Self-examination with feelings of guilt or shame
		3. A critical assessment of epistemic, sociocultural, or psychic assumptions
		4. Recognition that one's discontent and the process of transformation are shared and that others have negotiated a similar change
	Deliberate	
Strategy	Learn content	5. Exploration of options for new roles, relationships, and actions
		6. Planning of a course of action
		7a. Acquisition of knowledge and skills for implementing one's plans
	Deliberate	
Act	Learn in action	7b. Acquisition of knowledge and skills for implementing one's plans
		8. Provisional trying of new roles
		9. Building of competence and self-confidence in new roles and relationships
Accept new perspective	New perspective	10. A reintegration into one's life on the basis of conditions dictated by one's new perspective.

LGBTQ Transformative Learning Model

The LGBTQ TL Model blends Mezirow's ten stages with an extracted outline of Wishik and Pierce's to create an interactive process of shifting and framing perspectives or themes (Table 2.1). The foundation for the proposed process provides insight into the critical questioning, learning about self and others, and the process of deliberation that may be missing from other conceptualizations prevalent in counseling and psychology.

Furthermore, these LGBTQ TL Model process stages—Question, Risk, Strategy, Act, and Accept New Perspective (QRSAA) stages—are repeated as adults experience four potential framing perspectives: LGBTQ Exists, Coming Out to Yourself, Coming Out to Others, and Valuing and Embracing Different Journeys (see Figure 2.1). The framing perspectives identify major themes of understanding that LGBTQ individuals construct and may hold from one time or another as they cope with sexual identity development within a heteronormative society. The arrows pointing at the figure represent heteronormative expectations and messages that continually confront the LGBTQ adult. This explanation recognizes that for some individuals, a change could be a first-order or major perspective transformation, and for others it could be a second-order change, which is less fundamental to the core of the individual's identity. LGBTQ adults also may continue a QRSAA process as they learn about and critically examine concepts and situations throughout their lives without necessarily resulting in these specific major perspective transformations.

For some people, there are external or internal catalytic events or moments (Donnelly, 2001) that culminate each sequence and commence a framing perspective. In other instances, people may just start to question the many personal and societal assumptions that surround them over time, with no one particular event catalyzing the experience.

Figure 2.1. Proposed LGBTQ TL Model: Process and Framing

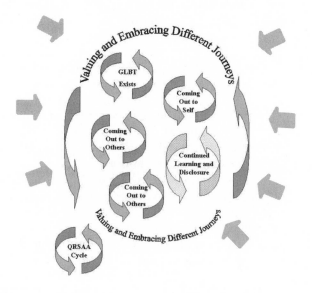

Source: King (2003).

These framing perspectives have webbed relationships that are not simply linear, normative, or progressive, but indicate a shifting back and forth through the QRSAA process and among the perspectives. This dynamic and structure emphasize the fact that LGBTQ individuals may never finish dealing with any of these issues. For instance, LGBTQ adults never cease coming out, but instead face the choice to do so daily. Each coming out is dealt with through new understandings, contexts, and decisions. Also, all the experiences are contributing toward the development of a holistic and overarching perspective of valuing and embracing different journeys rather than describing a linear development of stages.

The progression of critical reflection, deliberation, learning, and action is an iterative cycle that moves toward each framing perspective. All individuals have their own journeys that unfold in their understanding, experience, and timeline. And even as one reaches the integrated perspective of valuing and embracing diversity, freedom to explore further understanding along the journey provides room for LGBTQ adults to never have to separate desire and sexuality (Lemert, 1996, in Brooks and Edwards, 1999), but instead continually, reflectively, and authentically explore new understandings and constructions for themselves.

Individuals have their own context, personality, and personal costs to navigate, and caution should be used against developing normative expectations and experiences (Brooks and Edwards, 1997; Hill, 1996). In addition, the results can have as many variations as in queer theory, which does not define a unified homosexual identity (Brooks and Edwards, 1999; Hill, 1996). With this in mind, broad strokes of the images of each perspective are offered here to provide a structure for consideration. These perspectives can be used to guide adults in considering their own journey and helping them to understand those of others:

• *LGBTQ exists.* In this perspective, the adult becomes aware of LGBTQ individuals and goes through questioning their understanding, considering the risk of pursuing answers and making decisions, developing strategies for dealing with possible new perspectives, and then acting and accepting the new "framing" perspective.

• *Coming out to yourself.* Within this experience, LGBTQ adults are wrestling with their personal sexual identity and whether they are in fact LGBTQ. Self-doubt, fear, risk, exhilaration, excitement, and potential can variously characterize this perspective.

• *Coming out to others.* The LGBTQ adult faces a lifelong question of when and where to come out to other people. In a society that increasingly treats coming out as a moment of revelation, public announcement, and climax, the reality is that many continually cope with coming out through assumptions about their presumed heterosexuality that are pressed on them from many directions. What does this tell me about how others may

New Directions for Adult and Continuing Education • DOI: 10.1002/ace

respond to me? Multiple experiences of this cycle may occur across the life span; hence, more than one cycle is included in Figure 2.1.

• *Valuing and embracing different journeys.* As LGBTQ adults resolve their sexual identity and coming out within themselves and to others, they can continue the journey by looking at varying experiences. Rather than becoming rigid in their own "LGBTQness," they have an opportunity to develop a more integrated perspective of sexual identity.

Coping with more than individuation and young adulthood, LGBTQ adults have many more issues, dynamics, and risks to consider as they wrestle with their own understanding, acceptance, and decisions regarding coming out throughout their adult lives. Within a heteronormative society, marginalization is a continuing force in the sexual identity development of gay and lesbian adults, and even more pronounced for bisexual and transgendered adults. Attention is drawn to how LGBTQ adults continually need to cope with and navigate these forces. The model provides a basis for validating the individual's questions and contexts, suggesting new directions, and providing a basis for further dialogue about the many diverse experiences of this journey.

Applying the LGBTQ TL Model to the Workplace

Taking this model further is to consider how it interfaces with the workplace. In particular, one has to consider coming out to self and coming out to others. LGBTQ adults have to come to grips with both of these issues at different times and perhaps several times in multiple settings. They realize as they go through their different career stages that the need to understand self, adult development, and their identity as sexual minorities is complicated with the possibility of their own homophobia and the certainty of societal homophobia. This model offers a basis to reflect on the personal journey of sexual identity development and internalize a coping process.

The following workplace scenarios are offered as illustrations of some dilemmas that LGBTQ adults face.

Support from the Straight-But-Not-Narrow Crowd. Missy was out at work and kept pictures of her partner, Kelly, and their children on her desk. Most people at the company knew Missy was a lesbian, and Kelly had accompanied Missy to the company's holiday party last year. But this year, as National Coming Out Day (October 11) approached, Missy decided she wanted to wear a button to work that day to publicize the event. When the day arrived, Missy not only wore a button that highlighted Coming Out Day, she brought to work a small selection of political, feminist, and LGBTQ buttons she and Kelly had collected over the years to show a few of her coworkers. Much to Missy's surprise, several coworkers asked if they could wear one of the buttons in support of her and of LGBTQ issues. She thought they were just joking, but several women and one man wanted to wear a political or LGBTQ button to make a point that day. At the end of the day, most reported that other coworkers, knowing that they were not gay or lesbian, looked amused at the buttons but said little. Others laughed and asked where they got the buttons. A male colleague who wore a button reported being haggled a bit by a few other men at work and that he did not realize how awkward this new type of interaction with his coworkers would feel for him. In fact, it made him question his own thoughts about how open he thought these colleagues really were.

Coming Out for the Holidays. Tom, age twenty-seven, started a new job recently, and although he had come out to his family some five years earlier, he had never been out in the workplace. However, since coming out to his family and building a relationship with his partner, Everett, Tom had started to feel more comfortable about his sexuality and whom he told of his relationship. Being comfortable with being out at work and in public became compelling to Tom as he moved along his own personal journey of coming out.

Since he and Everett had relocated, Tom was starting with a clean slate at work; no one knew about his family or his life partner. This reality became evident as coworkers began talking about their plans for the holiday season with their families. Tom's coworkers began to ask him about his holiday plans, and for the first time in his life, Tom hesitated—not because he was falling into his old pattern of deflecting the issue and talking about his family in a more generic way; it was because he felt out of place for not talking about Everett. Tom realized that he wanted to share his plans with his coworkers because he was proud of his relationship, and he wanted to feel as legitimate as those around him. Instead of finishing Tom's story here, the more appropriate questions in this context might be, "How can the workplace support all LGBTQ employees, let alone be aware of and support someone like Tom?"

Deconstructing the Scenarios: The LGBTQ TL Model. The LGBTQ TL Model offers a way to deconstruct the situations described and other adults' experiences, to look at the values and beliefs that are underlying behavior and consider whether they are still valid for the individual, and to question whether they still want to hold onto them and endure the consequences. It also offers a way to consider if they want to explore a new perspective and once they try it, to consider if it fits them and whether they should keep it.

The model provides a framework to work through the inner dimensions intellectually ("I can work through and understand"), emotionally ("I can know my feelings and feel the experience to the outer dimensions"), and socially ("I can interact").

Career Stages

Another level of application and discussion is how sexual identity development interweaves with career development (see Chapter Three, this vol-

New Directions for Adult and Continuing Education • DOI: 10.1002/ace

ume). As professionals, adults go through many stages as they prepare, search, interview, start, and then progress from novice to experienced and advanced professional. Along the way, they usually gain additional work responsibilities, and their work may change significantly in the type of task they are assigned—from staff to manager, for instance. Further dimensions of variation are certain in this new millennium as adults experience on the average five or six career changes in their life spans.

Add to these certain changes and adjustments in any adult's life the LGBTQ sexual identity development in the workplace, and you have multiple strands of adjustment, relationships, disclosure, learning, and uncertainty careening. The LGBTQ TL Model provides a basis for dissecting these multiple strands and sorting through coping with them from the inside out. Moving to the point of application, we now turn to recommendations for facilitating this model in workplace training.

Facilitating the LGBTQ TL Model in the Workplace

In the workplace, training using the LGBTQ TL Model can be facilitated in a variety of ways. First, introducing the need and issues surrounding LGBTQ adult sexual identity is important and can be presented using many different instructional techniques. Here is the opportunity to model and explore an understandable process for adults to think about LGBTQ sexual identity situations. Among techniques that may be especially comfortable to use are scenarios like those above and media articles and video clips to explore current situations and issues that surround the particular context of this group of adults. Building on environments of respect and safety, adult educators and organizations can serve as catalysts to broaden discussions in families, communities, and classrooms to include considering, valuing, and embracing varied understandings of sexual identities. Mining these experiences, we can provide space and permission for adults to begin or continue to integrate their desires and sexuality in their lives. Feminist pedagogy has provided a tradition of examining and learning from personal experience in the light of power and oppression. Queer theory now extends critical theory and feminist pedagogy to question normative definitions of sexual identity (Brooks and Edwards, 1999). Benefits are therefore possible not only for individuals but also for our workplaces, community, and society.

Second, several additional instructional techniques in small group formats can be used to introduce and explore the LGBTQ TL Model. The model can be introduced with a minimum of theory and an emphasis on illustration of mainstream adult learning and change experiences, while drawing understanding and parallels with which the greatest number of people can identify. This may be done in handouts, short presentations, and jigsaw assignments in which different aspects of the model are assigned to groups to present. Narratives and role playing can be used to explore the meaning of the model and examine its application in general settings.

Finally, the model can be more specifically applied to LGBTQ workplace situations to determine how adults may experience issues, concerns, and conflicts. Personal, professional, and academic research regarding these experiences may use narratives and dialogue as natural vehicles to help LGBTQ adults reflect on and process these experiences as they continue on their journeys. They can also be used as heterosexual adults "take on the role of the other" in mind and consider their needs and conflicts (Brooks and Edwards, 1997; Donnelly, 2001). In addition, facilitators can use case studies, role playing, critical incidents, extended discussions, and journaling to allow individuals to document their perceptions of current situations at work, in the media and community, or at home on these issues.

In all of these strategies, questioning, which allows adults to think about the issues carefully and with concern for themselves and others, may include: What can I learn from my own sexual identity journey? Where am I on this journey? Were the risks great or small for me? What helped me face the risks? What made it difficult? What strategies did I consider? Were LGBTQ individuals always visible to me? How did I respond? What can I do to support others along their journey?

Conclusion

The LGBTQ TL Model provides a perspective and coping strategies for LGBTQ adults to frame their journey of sexual identity development. These can be juxtaposed with the ways in which the LGBTQ population may confront hostile workplaces provided by Muñoz and Thomas (see Chapter Eight, this volume). Rather than seeing their experiences as isolated, they can see the commonalities. Because of their subordinate sexual orientation (Wishik and Pierce, 1991), LGBTQ adults must deal with their sexual identity on a daily basis in the workplace in ways that heterosexual adults do not have to. Instead of seeing a single dimension of the sexual identity question, this model highlights multiple layers and many conflicts through which LGBTQ adults must learn to move daily in their blended personal and professional lives.

The LGBTQ TL Model and related instructional strategies provide a framework to approach these daily challenges and questions through a critically reflective, transformative learning lens that builds greater understanding of self, sexual identity, societal expectations, and colleagues and provides space and freedom to question these assumptions. As LGBTQ individuals and allies consider these questions together, new constructions of understanding and acceptance may be created. Each of us has the opportunity to come to new understandings and insights regarding ourselves, those like us, and those different from ourselves. Gaining a framework of development and enveloping it with critical questioning, concern, and acceptance provides a basis for adults to construct their sexual identity in a place of safety and respect and to develop lifelong coping skills to meet the continuing challenges that life will bring. By bringing such learning to the workplace,

New Directions for Adult and Continuing Education • DOI: 10.1002/ace

we offer the opportunity to create a safer environment in which professionals may work and grow.

References

Brooks, A. K., and Edwards, K. "Narratives of Women's Sexual Identity Development." In R. Nolan and H. Chelesvig (eds.), *Thirty-Eighth Annual Adult Education Research Conference Proceedings.* Stillwater: Oklahoma State University, 1997. (ED 409 460)

Brooks, A. K., and Edwards, K. "For Adults Only: Queer Theory Meets the Self and Identity in Adult Education." In A. Rose (ed.), *Fortieth Annual Adult Education Research Conference Proceedings.* DeKalb: Northern Illinois University, 1999. (ED 431 901)

Cass, V. "Homosexual Identity Formation: Testing a Theoretical Model." *Journal of Sex Research,* 1984, 20(2), 143–167.

"Court Annuls San Francisco Gay Marriages." MSNBC, Aug. 12, 2004. http://www.msnbc.msn.com/id/5685429/print/1/displaymode/1098/. Accessed Nov. 15, 2005.

Cranton, P. *Understanding and Promoting Transformative Learning.* San Francisco: Jossey-Bass, 1994.

Donnelly, S. *Building a New Moral, Religious, or Spiritual Identity: Perspective Transformation in Lesbian Women.* San Antonio: Texas A&M University, 2001.

Hill, R. "Learning to Transgress: A Sociohistorical Conspectus of the American Gay Lifeworld as a Site of Struggle and Resistance." *Studies in the Education of Adults,* 1996, 28(2), 253–279.

King, K. P. "Changing from the Inside Out." In. R. Hill (ed.), *The Adult Education Research Conference LGBTQ&A Caucus Preconference.* San Francisco: San Francisco State University, 2003.

King, K. P. *Bringing Transformative Learning to Life.* Malabar, Fla.: Krieger, 2005.

Mezirow, J. *Education for Perspective Transformation.* New York: Teachers College, Columbia University, 1978.

Mezirow, J. *Transformative Dimensions of Adult Learning.* San Francisco: Jossey-Bass, 1991.

Mezirow, J., and Associates. *Fostering Critical Reflection in Adulthood.* San Francisco: Jossey-Bass, 1990.

Mezirow, J., and Associates. *Learning as Transformation.* San Francisco: Jossey-Bass, 2000.

"Neighbors Denounce Anti-gay Hate Crime." *People's Weekly World Newspaper Online,* July 7, 2005. http://www.pww.org/article/articleview/7355/1/277/. Accessed Nov. 14, 2005.

"San Francisco Weds Gay Couples." CNN, Feb. 12, 2004. http://www.cnn.com/2004/LAW/02/12/gay.marriage.california.ap. Accessed Nov. 13, 2005.

Taylor, B. "'Coming Out' as a Life Transition: Homosexual Identity Formation and Its Implications for Health Care Practice." *Journal of Advanced Nursing,* 1999, 30(2), 520–525.

Wishik, H., and Pierce, C. *Sexual Orientation and Identity: Heterosexual, Lesbian, Gay, and Bisexual Journeys.* Laconia, N.H.: New Dynamics, 1991.

KATHLEEN P. KING *is professor of adult education in the Graduate School of Education and director of the Regional Educational Technology Center at Fordham University, New York.*

SUSAN C. BIRO *is associate director of the Regional Educational Technology Center at Fordham University, New York.*

3

This chapter deconstructs heterosexual privilege in the workplace and offers suggestions for "queering the workplace" with an emphasis on career development.

Straight Privilege and Moral/izing: Issues in Career Development

Tonette S. Rocco, Suzanne J. Gallagher

This chapter discusses and explores straight privilege and moralizing and the effects of straight privilege on the career development of LGBTQ people. We begin with a discussion of heterosexism, moralizing, privilege, and the resultant discrimination. Next, using career construction theory (Super, 1990), we deconstruct heterosexual privilege as it relates to the career development of LGBTQ people. From this we move to a discussion of queering career development and implications for adult education.

To us, *queering career development* means that at the individual level, both heterosexuals and LGBTQ people need to reflect on heterosexist privilege. Heterosexuals must recognize heterosexism and its negative effects in the workplace. For instance, discrimination that LGBTQ people regularly experience results in decreased participation, causing their knowledge and abilities to become wasted resources.

The term *moral/izing* is constructed with a slash purposefully. The use of the symbol / is a device commonly employed in writing influenced by notions of poststructural hyphenation. It signals to the reader that she or he must rework the term in deconstructive ways. Slashed words thus become compound words in a complex manner. Here, *moral/izing* implies a value-laden process that distinguishes "morals" from "moralizing." Hill (2005) argues that the former can be an essential and constructive ingredient in the sociocultural formation of people and groups. The latter, however, often is destructive insofar as it universalizes *specific* (conservative and fundamentalist) morals and imposes them on others as the only way in which to mediate life.

NEW DIRECTIONS FOR ADULT AND CONTINUING EDUCATION, no. 112, Winter 2006 © 2006 Wiley Periodicals, Inc.
Published online in Wiley InterScience (www.interscience.wiley.com) • DOI: 10.1002/ace.234

Revealing Heterosexism, Moralizing, and Heterosexual Privilege

The interlocking dynamics of heterosexism, moralizing, and privilege result in discrimination against LGBTQ people. Through defining the terms, the multiple layers and places where discrimination exists become evident.

Heterosexism. Heterosexism, or heterosexual privilege, is a system of oppression that reduces the experience of sexual minorities to medical or criminal causes while victimizing people who are seen as sexual minorities through violence or diminished opportunity. "Heterosexism sustains a legal system that denies equal protection and property rights (such as marriage) and holds in contempt the personal relationships of sexual minorities" (Rocco and Gallagher, 2006, p. 11).

The term *straight* refers to heterosexual people and "is being used here as someone who has *never* engaged in deviant or outlaw sexual behavior and sexual acts are *only* with an opposite sex partner. In this definition of straight, a person only engages in sexual activity with opposite sex partners throughout the lifespan" (Rocco and Gallagher, 2006, p. 12), which is rare. *Lesbian, gay, bisexual, transgender, and queer* (LGBTQ) refers to people who have sexual and personal relationships or possess an identity that is outside the heterosexual norm, for example, transgender people. "'Transgender' has become an umbrella term representing a political alliance between all gender variant people who do not conform to social norms for typical men and women and who suffer political oppression as a result" (*GLBTQ Encyclopedia,* 2004). One group under the transgender umbrella is intersexed people: "Intersexuals are people born physically between the male and female genders with anatomy that is either ambiguous or comprised of varying degrees of both male and female anatomy" (ITPeople, 2005).

The term *queer* is being used to encompass all the variations in sexual desire, activity, and identity that are not straight. *Queer* is also used by LGBTQ people as a way to create an identity as a community. Some authors, including Hill (2004, p. 85), use "*queer* to describe a particular form of political dissidence that blurs the dominant binary gender distinction of male and female."

Moralizing and Discrimination. Moral, ethical, and practical reasons support the need to examine and deconstruct heterosexism or straight privilege. Morals are socially defined and context specific. Consider the widely held family value of racism or white privilege in the pre–Civil War era that blacks should be enslaved. Slavery was based on the moral position that white slave owners were human and needed to care for their black captives, who were viewed as animal-like in their simplicity (Smiley, 2004). This racism has had emotional, political, and economic impacts on African Americans. In much the same way, there are long-term effects on adults who as children realized they were attracted to same-sex friends or their sexual orientation was not what was discussed as "normal" in their families, a phenomenon that stigmatizes them and limits their career and life options.

Heterosexism maintains moral superiority of heterosexuals over LGBTQ people based on a notion that "normal" sex is activity between a man and a woman. Moralizing defines the directional use of power by heterosexuals through the predominance of heterosexism and homonegativity, or negative thoughts, feelings, and behaviors toward LGBTQ people (Alderson, 2003). This is supported by the myth of choice—that LGBTQ people choose this "lifestyle" and are therefore immoral. Heterosexism ignores the fact that no straight person makes a conscious decision or choice to be straight. Instead, straight people claim moral superiority and build on this foundation a system of emotional, political, and economic oppression that acts to deny full citizenship to LGBTQ people (Richardson, 1998).

Citizenship includes civil or legal rights, political rights, and social rights (Marshall, 1950, as cited in Richardson, 1998). For LGBTQ people, civil rights should include the right to inherit from a partner or to have the relationship legally sanctioned. Political rights include voting, which LGBTQ people are not denied. Although the right to serve in the military can be denied if sexual minority status is not well hidden, this career choice for LGBTQ people is perilous. Social rights include economic security and to be part of the community. Economic security is diminished by a lack of civil and political rights. Employment discrimination based on sexual minority status is legal in many places in the United States (see Chapter Seven, this volume).

"Statewide protections against workplace discrimination exist in only 16 states; in the rest of the country, employees fired for being gay have no legal recourse unless they work in a locality with its own anti-discrimination ordinance" (Lambda Legal, 2006). Institutionalized forms of discrimination have economic consequences for the victims and society. The victims earn less and therefore make reduced contributions to the tax base than they might have otherwise.

Privilege and Discrimination. The framework for privilege used here is based on a triarchy of privilege where the psychosocial, reciprocal, and structural realms are interlocked and result in discriminatory beliefs, practices, and policies (Rocco and West, 1998). *Psychosocial* "refers to internalized uncritical acceptance of assumptions gained through socialization" (Rocco and West, 1998, p. 176). Internalization of these assumptions becomes tacit knowledge that can be out of sync with our espoused beliefs. Overcoming the assumption that being LGBTQ is immoral, LGBTQ people spend an inordinate amount of time and energy wrestling with their sexual identity, often interrupting or delaying their career development (Boatwright, Gilbert, Forrest, and Ketzenberger, 1996). For instance, some LGBTQ people become deeply religious while trying to come to terms with or deny their minority sexual status, considering religious life as a career. Or they dismiss other career options because of the fear that a felt or preferred vocation would be too dangerous, such as becoming a teacher.

The reciprocal realm comprises our interactions with others. Privileged people can choose not to fight discrimination and unjust social relationships (Wildman, Armstrong, Davis, and Grillo, 1996). Heterosexuals have the privilege of ignoring differences in sexual orientation. "The holder of privilege need not feel excluded when the norm describes her own actuality" as is the case with heterosexuals who do not see their privilege (Wildman, 1996, p. 30). Privilege results in a greater social comfort for heterosexuals and requires no or less energy to manage one's sexual identity in relation to the workplace. Heterosexuals do not have to continually evaluate the safety of disclosing their sexual identity or coming out to others (Allen, 1995; Sedgwick, 1993). In everyday conversations, for instance, when colleagues discuss what they did over the weekend and with whom they did an activity, decisions about how much to disclose and whether to disclose at all must be made. A worker who lives in constant fear that someone will find out that he or she is an LGBTQ (or other sexual minority, such as intersexuals) takes energy away from productive activities.

The structural realm is reflected in a consistent history of "norms, policies, and language which maintain and sanction" (Rocco and West, 1998, p. 177) the status of the dominant culture. "Privilege is the systematic conferral of benefit and advantage" (Wildman, 1996, p. 29). For example, "the failure of the U.S. Congress to pass the Employment Discrimination Act attests to the lack of acceptance for the needs of gay men and lesbian women in the workplace" (Pope and others, 2004, p. 159). The invisibility of privilege in the workplace maintains systems of discrimination and ensures the replication of LGBTQ people's subordination (Wildman, 1996). This subordination is illustrated when a supervisor fires a worker simply because he is gay or she is a lesbian. Discrimination based on sexual orientation is not protected by federal law. (For a fuller discussion of this point, see Chapter Seven, this volume.)

Heterosexist privilege causes LGBTQ people to make a choice to pass as straight at different times. The concept of choosing to pass as straight may not be a choice at all if the person's economic survival or family relationships are based on keeping one's sexual identity secret. As Sedgwick (1993, p. 46) reminds us, "even at an individual level, there are remarkably few of even the most openly gay people who are not deliberately in the closet with someone personally or economically or institutionally important to them," or, we might add, with power over them. For every new introduction or encounter, a decision is made about how much to disclose, when to disclose, and what the consequences are if the decision to disclose was ill advised or the wrong decision.

Career Development

Career development theory has evolved from its vocational development roots into career construction theory (Savickas, 2002). Vocational development theory focuses on matching personality traits to occupational requirements (Parsons, 1909, as cited in Savickas, 2002). Super (1990) advanced a career construction theory that focuses on an individual's adaptive patterns regarding work and the construction of a vocational self-concept. Self-concept is "a picture of the self in some role, situation, or position, performing some set of functions, or in some web of relationships" (Super, 1963, p. 18). Career construction theory is "more attuned to conceptualizing development as driven by adaptation to an environment than by maturation of inner structures" (Savickas, 2002, p. 154). Career construction theory allows us to see the interactions between social patterns and the individual's self-concept.

Consistent with the career construction theory, Hall's definition of career (2002) reflects the subjective orientation of career development theory: "The career is the individually perceived sequence of attitudes and behaviors associated with work-related experiences and activities over the span of the person's life" (Hall, 2002, p. 12). Missing from this definition is the sociological view of career development where educational opportunities, socioeconomic status, race, and gender influence career development (Hotchkiss and Borow, 1996). The definition is also limited by the exclusion of sexual identity. A holistic view of career development includes both the individual's experience and an analysis of contextual issues that affect the development of one's vocation.

Super (1990) introduced the tradition of a series of segmented processes in career development for research and theoretical development. The segmented processes of career development include choice, establishment, advancement, maintenance, and work/life issues:

• "Choosing employment" includes identifying the type of work and a specific organization. Career choices are influenced by a constellation of relationships and their effect on vocational identity development (Hall, 2002). They are often made more than once in a lifetime.

• "Establishment" means entering and adjusting to the workplace. It includes initial training and orientation, setting up one's work space, and building relationships within the workplace.

• "Advancement," an increase in status, salary, and scope of responsibility, relies on performance, networking, mentoring, and access to formal and informal training.

• "Management" is dealing with changes in the workplace or in one's career. It includes the evolving construction of self-concept, changes in leadership, and adapting to new coworkers and working conditions.

• "Work/life issues" are issues affected by career activity but not occurring within the workplace. Examples are significant relationships, families, births, adoptions, vacations, illness, formal schooling, citizenship, and lifestyles (such as exercise, eating habits, and leisure choices).

Choosing, establishment, advancement, management, and work/life issues will serve as focus areas for deconstructing straight privilege in career development.

Deconstructing Straight Privilege in Career Development

In this section, we analyze the five focus areas of career development—choice, establishment, advancement, maintenance, and work/life issues—through the psychosocial, reciprocal, and structural realms of privilege. In addition we provide examples of overt and covert discrimination in each of the five areas (Chojnacki and Gelberg, 1994).

Choosing. Choosing employment includes identifying the type of work and an organization. Selecting a career involves more than personality fit for LGBTQ people. LGBTQ workers are attracted to occupations and organizations that are gay friendly (Friskopp and Silverstein, 1995). "A gay worker will avoid occupations in which either (1) is relatively difficult to pass as heterosexual, or (2) the penalties for disclosure of a gay identity are relatively high because of institutional policies or co-worker attitudes" (Badgett and King, 1997, p. 75).

One study found that lesbians limited their job choices to avoid heterosexist work environments (Fassinger, 1996). The psychosocial cost of heterosexism, for example, delayed the decision of one of us to pursue a doctorate because of the fear of being found out as a lesbian and the potential of being fired after securing a faculty position.

Establishment. Establishment means entering and adjusting to the workplace. The workplace includes individual, communal, and organizational work spaces that must be traversed, including the rules for safe social engagement.

Individual spaces such as the cubicle or private office may be devoid of family pictures or personal memorabilia that disclose one's sexual identity. Individual spaces are rarely private. Coworkers may ask why a colleague does not display pictures or stop by to chat, innocently inquiring about the previous night's activity, an inquiry that could have negative consequences if addressed honestly. In fact, secrecy around a personal life can be misunderstood by colleagues and delay or prevent promotions.

Communal spaces such as lunch rooms contain the angst of deciding how much to disclose in conversation (Allen, 1995). Bathrooms contain more specific risks from homophobic colleagues who will scurry out of the bathroom if an openly LGBTQ coworker steps inside. Transgender people must expend energy contemplating which bathroom to use. Gay rights organizations state that transgender individuals should use the bathroom that corresponds to the gender he or she identifies with, not the biological sex at birth. The Legal Aid Society Employment Division states that "courts and administrative bodies throughout the country—including California—have recognized that discrimination against transgender and gender non-conforming people is a form of sex discrimination" (Harris and Minter, 2002).

Organizational spaces include the organizational culture, human resource policies and procedures, and access to training and mentoring, which are dominated by heterosexism. For instance, diversity training may not include the experiences of LGBTQ people as part of the definition of diversity. Some organizational cultures, such as the military, foster the notion that LGBTQ people reduce morale and are sexually aggressive and indiscreet.

Work spaces are infused with the expectation and assumption of heterosexuality and the repression of nonheterosexual behavior (Boatwright, Gilbert, Forrest, and Ketzenberger, 1996) requiring constant monitoring, indirect conversation (use of pronouns), and isolation on the part of LGBTQ people. The invisibility of sexual orientation as opposed to race or gender increases the fear of sexual minorities because they may not be seen and therefore controlled. Between 25 and 66 percent of gay and lesbians experience workplace discrimination (Ragins and Wiethoff, 2005). Discrimination against LGBTQ people and those perceived to be LGBTQ is still legal in the majority of workplaces (Ragins and Wiethoff, 2005). For example, Cheryl Summerville, a former cook at a Cracker Barrel restaurant, was fired for "failing to comply with normal heterosexual values" (Gold, 2001, p. 163). If an LGBTQ person can "pass," or hide his or her minority sexual status, secrecy and social distance must be maintained from other employees, which comes at a high psychological cost (Badgett and King, 1997). The psychological cost includes the pressure to pass and the lack of social support. In addition, "heterosexuals may avoid associating with gay and lesbian coworkers because they fear that they will be perceived as being gay" (Ragins and Wiethoff, 2005, p. 182). Being perceived as being gay increases the "courtesy stigmas," or discrimination against people who associate with minorities. Courtesy stigmas do not occur on the basis of gender and less frequently on the basis of race (Goffman, 1963). The fear that some heterosexuals of being labeled because of association have increases the isolation of LGBTQ people at work and decreases their ability to form meaningful and productive work relationships.

Advancement. Advancement is an increase in status, salary, and scope of responsibility. Friskopp and Silverstein (1995) found that heterosexism limits the career advancement of gay men and lesbians. Corporations and even gay executives preferred LGBTQ people to stay in the closet (Miller, 1995). Workplace heterosexism resulted in fewer promotions over a ten-year period for LGBTQ people (Ragins and Cornwell, 2001). In the workplace, people who hold heterosexist beliefs help gay and lesbians less than those who are not heterosexist (Ellis and Fox, 2001). The effects of heterosexism are evident: less access to mentoring and therefore fewer opportunities for advancement.

Management. Management is dealing with changes in the workplace or one's career. An important issue for LGBTQ people is which people at work to disclose to. The process of coming out to others at work adds stress to the LGBTQ person's work experience because this process requires weighing the risks against the benefits and making hard choices. LGBTQ people have to discover who is safe to come out to and if that person will tell people who are heterosexist or unsafe. This process consumes mental and emotional energy and may detract from performance. The LGBTQ person who is wrong in assessing a person's safety risks losing his or her job, supportive relationships of mentors, role models and peers, and career advancement opportunities.

Workplaces that lack antidiscrimination policies and practices may foster an atmosphere of heterosexism (Button, 2001). Ragins and Wiethoff reported that "heterosexism had a negative relationship with job satisfaction, organizational commitment, career commitment, organization-based self-esteem, and satisfaction with opportunities for promotion" (Ragins and Wiethoff, 2005, p. 187).

Even with gay-friendly policies, company practices may promote heterosexism. The best indicator of a nonheterosexist work environment was being able to invite same-sex partners to company social events (Ragins and Cornwell, 2001).

Work/Life Roles. Work/life issues are those affected by career activity but not occurring within the workplace. Unlike the experience of racial minorities with a strong family support system who have encountered and managed discrimination based on race, people with differing sexual orientations may have little to no family support (Ragins and Wiethoff, 2005). Their family members may share little common knowledge of LGBTQ issues and may be struggling with their own heterosexist baggage. Families still disown their sexual minority relatives or ostracize them in other ways. Some families seek to support their sexual minority relatives but do so without actually having experience with discrimination based on sexual orientation. Additional stress on the job and lack of social support increase the risk of substance abuse or unhealthy lifestyles such as promiscuity (Ragins and Wiethoff, 2005). Partners of LGBTQ people may be excluded from conversations around the proverbial watercooler or may be uninvited to company functions in order to maintain the safe space at work for the LGBTQ person. Illness, death, births, and adoptions are difficult terrain for LGBTQ people to navigate in heterosexist workplaces.

Queering Career Development

The question is how to create nondiscriminatory or queer work environments for heterosexual and GLBTQ people. Developing queer work environments requires interventions at the individual, program, and advocacy levels.

New Directions for Adult and Continuing Education • DOI: 10.1002/ace

LGBTQ people should learn to identify the effects of heterosexism on their career development—for instance, loss of productivity and lack of access. They also need to learn to build other networks and support systems to counter the potentially debilitating pain caused by the hateful acts of others; this is another means to queer career development.

At the program level within the organization, "didactic information is helpful in challenging heterosexist assumptions but generally is insufficient; experiential and cognitive components are superior" (Simoni and Walters, 2001, p. 13). The value of LGBTQ people coming out to themselves and others is significant. Research has shown a correlation between the level of engagement with gay and lesbians and the level of heterosexism. Increased contact with self-identifying LBGTQ people results in decreased heterosexism (Herek, 1990). In order to create a safe space, organizations need to have policies in place to combat heterosexist language, jokes, and remarks (Friskopp and Silverstein, 1995), as well as nondiscriminatory policies.

At the advocacy or social level, nondiscriminatory legislation, including legislation for equal benefits and legal protections, is essential to queering career development. Notions of alternative family arrangements, gay rights, and civil unions, among other issues, influence the career choices and development of LGBTQ people.

Creating queer work spaces means challenging relationships that are not generative or caring, or naming the dynamics, the actions, and the meanings that are discriminatory and oppressive. Queer work spaces challenge privilege that creates oppressive relationships at work to make heterosexual and LGBTQ persons' career development equitable.

References

Alderson, K. G. "The Corporate Closet: Career Challenges of Gay and Lesbian Individuals." Paper presented at the Annual National Consultation on Career Development Convention, Ottawa, Ontario. Jan. 20–23, 2003.

Allen, K. R. "Opening the Classroom Closet: Sexual Orientation and Self-Disclosure." *Family Relations*, 1995, 44(2), 136–141.

Badgett, M.V.L., and King, M. C. "Lesbian and Gay Occupational Strategies." In A. Gluckman and B. Reed (eds.), *HomoEconomics: Capitalism, Community, and Lesbian and Gay Life*. New York: Routledge, 1997.

Boatwright, K. J., Gilbert, M. S., Forrest L., and Ketzenberger, K. "Impact of Identity Development upon Career Trajectory: Listening to the Voices of Lesbian Women." *Journal of Vocational Behavior*, 1996, 48, 210–228.

Button, S. B. "Organizational Efforts to Affirm Sexual Diversity: A Cross-Level Examination." *Journal of Applied Psychology*, 2001, 86, 17–28.

Chojnacki, J. T., and Gelberg, S. "Toward a Conceptualization of Career Counseling with Gay/Lesbian/Bisexual Persons." *Journal of Career Development*, 1994, 21, 3–10.

Ellis, J., and Fox, P. "The Effect of Self-Identified Sexual Orientation on Helping Behavior in a British Sample: Are Lesbians and Gay Men Treated Differently?" *Journal of Applied Social Psychology*, 2001, 31, 1238–1247.

Fassinger, R. E. "Notes from the Margins: Integrating Lesbian Experience into the Vocational Psychology of Women." *Journal of Vocational Behavior*, 1996, 48, 160–175.

Friskopp, A., and Silverstein, S. *Straight Jobs, Gay Lives.* New York: Scribner, 1995.

GLBTQ Encyclopedia. "Transgender." http://www.glbtq.com/social-sciences/transgender.html. 2004. Accessed June 25, 2005.

Goffman, E. *Behavior in Public Places.* New York: Free Press, 1963.

Gold, T. "Making Out at Work." In K. Krupat and P. McCreery (eds.), *Out at Work.* Minneapolis: University of Minnesota Press, 2001.

Hall, D. T. *Careers in and out of Organizations.* Thousand Oaks, Calif.: Sage, 2002.

Harris, S. I., and Minter, S. "Legal Translations: Employment Discrimination and the California Department of Fair Employment and Housing." *Bay Area Reporter,* July 11, 2002. http://www.las-elc.org/arch-020711-transgender.html. Accessed Sept. 21, 2006.

Herek, G. M. "The Context of Anti-Gay Violence: Notes on Cultural and Psychological Heterosexism." *Journal of Interpersonal Violence,* 1990, *5,* 316–333.

Hill, R. J. "Activism as Practice: Some Queer Considerations." In R. St. Clair and J. E. Sandlin (eds.), *Promoting Critical Practice in Adult Education.* New Directions for Adult and Continuing Education, no. 102. San Francisco: Jossey-Bass, 2004.

Hill, R. J. "AIDS, Empire and the Politics of Giving." *Convergence,* 2005, *37*(4), 59–73.

Hotchkiss, L., and Borow, H. "Sociological Perspectives on Work and Career Development." In D. Brown, L. Brooks, and Associates (eds.), *Career Choice and Development: Applying Contemporary Theories to Practice.* San Francisco: Jossey-Bass, 1996.

ITPeople. *Intersexed.* http://www.itpeople.org/intersexed.php. Accessed Oct. 20, 2005.

Lambda Legal. *Employment Issues.* http://www.lambdalegal.org/cgi-bin/iowa/index.html. Accessed May 12, 2006.

Miller, G. V. *The Gay Male Odyssey in the Corporate World: From Disempowerment to Empowerment.* New York: Harrington Park Press, 1995.

Parsons, F. *Choosing a Vocation.* New York: Agathon Press, 1909.

Pope, M., and others. "Culturally Appropriate Career Counseling with Gay and Lesbian Clients." *Career Development Quarterly,* 2004, *53*(2), 158–177.

Ragins, B. R., and Cornwell, J. M. "Pink Triangles: Antecedents and Consequences of Perceived Workplace Discrimination Against Gay and Lesbian Employees." *Journal of Applied Psychology,* 2001, *86,* 1244–1261.

Ragins, B. R., and Wiethoff, C. "Understanding Heterosexism at Work: The Straight Problem." In R. L. Dipboye and A. Colello (eds.), *Discrimination at Work.* Mahwah, N.J.: Erlbaum, 2005.

Richardson, D. "Sexuality and Citzenship." *Sociology,* 1998, *32*(1), 83–100.

Rocco, T. S., and Gallagher, S. "Straight Privilege, Moral/izing, and Myths: The Effects on Learners, Educational Options, and Teaching for Social Justice." Unpublished manuscript, 2006.

Rocco, T. S., and West, G. W. "Deconstructing Privilege: An Examination of Privilege in Adult Education." *Adult Education Quarterly,* 1998, *48*(3), 171–184.

Savickas, M. L. "Career Construction: A Developmental Theory of Vocational Behavior." In D. Brown (ed.), *Career Choice and Development.* (4th ed.) San Francisco: Jossey-Bass, 2002.

Sedgwick, E. K. "Epistemology of the Closet." In H. Abelove, M. A. Barale, and D. M. Halperin (eds.), *The Lesbian and Gay Studies Reader.* New York: Routledge, 1993.

Simoni, J. M., and Walters, K. L. "Heterosexual Identity and Heterosexism: Recognizing Privilege to Reduce Prejudice." *Journal of Homosexuality,* 2001, *41*(1), 157–172.

Smiley, T. "Interview with Jesse Jackson on The Tavis Smiley Show." Washington D.C.: National Public Radio and the African American Consortium. Nov. 4, 2004. Radio broadcast.

Super, D. E. *Career Development: Self-Concept Theory, Essays in Vocational Development.* New York: College Entrance Examination Board, 1963.

Super, D. E. "A Life-Span, Life Space to Career Development." In D. Brown, L. Brooks, and Associates (eds.), *Career Choice and Development*. (2nd ed.) San Francisco: Jossey-Bass, 1990.

Wildman, S. M., with Armstrong, M., Davis, A. D., and Grillo, T. *Privilege Revealed: How Invisible Preference Undermines America*. New York: New York University Press, 1996.

TONETTE S. ROCCO is an associate professor of adult education and human resource development at Florida International University.

SUZANNE J. GALLAGHER is an adjunct assistant professor at St. Thomas University.

4

This chapter explores the challenges and the opportunities that lesbians experience in organizational America.

Lesbians: Identifying, Facing, and Navigating the Double Bind of Sexual Orientation and Gender in Organizational Settings

Julie Gedro

Lesbians who work in corporate America face multiple challenges, which include sexual identity development, occupational and organizational selection, and sexual identity disclosure. They have to learn how to negotiate the heterosexism, homophobia, and sexism of their organizational settings in order to achieve success in their careers. Because the fields of adult education and human resource development (HRD) have paid little attention to studying lesbians and organizational settings, this chapter explores the unique issues related to lesbians in organizations and concludes with some ideas and suggestions for addressing these issues.

Organizational Hetereosexism, Heterosexist Organizational Privilege, and Homophobia

Organizational heterosexism is a system of hegemonic dominance that privileges heterosexuality as the only acceptable form of sexual or relational expression (Griffin, 1998). Heterosexist privilege is the taken-for-granted "rights" of straight people that allows them to choose, for example, whether to discuss their personal and family lives at work. Heterosexist privilege is a pervasive and ubiquitous assumption that the norm is for a person to be straight. Lesbians, gays, and bisexuals are considered to be sexual minori-

New Directions for Adult and Continuing Education, no. 112, Winter 2006 © 2006 Wiley Periodicals, Inc.
Published online in Wiley InterScience (www.interscience.wiley.com) • DOI: 10.1002/ace.235

ties who continue to face prejudice, oppression, and discrimination (Chung, 2001). Most organizations are dominated by a heterosexist, male power structure, which constructs lesbians and gay men as isolated exceptions whose sexualities are perceived to be "personal problems" (Burrell and Hearn, 1989, in Niesche, 2003, p. 44).

Homosexuality is the last acceptable prejudice. Considered sexual minorities, lesbians and gays continue to face discrimination, social oppression, and prejudice based on stereotypes, fear, and lack of education (Alderson, 2003; Chung, 2001; Levine and Leonard, 1984; Ragins, Cornwell, and Miller, 2003). In spite of diversity initiatives, intolerance of lesbian and gay people still exists in society and carries over into the workplace (Day and Schoenrade, 1997). Homophobia, an irrational fear and hatred of lesbians and gays, is a major aspect affecting lesbian and gay people because the lesbian and gay experience is seen as inferior, whereas heterosexuality is viewed as natural and normal (Fassinger, 1995). "Homophobia works effectively as a weapon of sexism because it is joined with a powerful arm, heterosexism" (Pharr, quoted in Heldke and O'Connor, 2004, p. 268). Prejudice against lesbians is grounded in sexism and misogyny (Miller, 1998), and the derision that is directed at lesbians is a result of the fact that lesbians have the "audacity to function without a man's support" (p. 25).

The Gap in Adult Education and HRD Around Issues Related to Lesbians

To be a lesbian is to be perceived as someone who has stepped out of line, who has moved out of sexual and economic dependence on a male, and who is woman identified (Pharr, quoted in Heldke and O'Conner, 2004). The career, business, management, and adult education fields have begun to pay attention to and research the experiences and learning of gays and lesbians in the world and in the workplace, in particular, in the corporate setting (Friskopp and Silverstein, 1995). There has been a lack of theory or research on the relationship between sexual orientation and other group memberships in the workplace (Ragins, Cornwell, and Miller, 2003). Lesbians who work in corporate America are paid little to no attention relative to their presence, experience, and learning. Multiple group membership, such as membership in a gender minority and sexual orientation minority, has been studied little (Ragins, Cornwell, and Miller, 2003). Rather than being considered a unique category of people with unique needs for learning, the lesbian experience is subsumed under either the literature and research on gay men or the literature and research on women. In addition, because there is a paucity of data and literature on them, lesbians must learn through trial and error how to negotiate their organizational settings.

Although work and careers are critical for lesbians, the field of psychology has traditionally paid little attention to the career counseling issues with them (Boatwright, Gilbert, Forrest, and Ketzenberger, 1996). HRD has paid little attention to issues affecting lesbian careers as well. Bierema (2002) noted that as a discipline, HRD "has not vigorously studied diversity, equality, power, heterosexism, discrimination, sexism, racism, or other issues of oppression in organizations" (p. 245). Bierema also noted that asymmetrical power arrangements are ignored in HRD research. Perhaps contributing to the lack of visibility in adult education and HRD research is the fact that lesbians are literally invisible in the corporate setting. Whereas one in seven gay men are recognizable as such to the general public, only one in twenty lesbians are recognizable (Button, 2004). Lesbians are more disadvantaged than gay men in organizations because it is possible for gay men to hide in the shadow of the dominant masculinity (Niesche, 2003). "Lesbians experience a double (for women of color, triple) minority status in the workplace and thus are subject to increased discrimination based on their multiple identities" (Garnets and Kimmel, quoted in Fassinger, 1995, p. 154).

The lack of attention to the lesbian experience in corporate America suggests that until now, the assumption has been that the experiences and needs of lesbians are subsumed under the study of the general female population (Morgan and Brown, 1991). Morgan and Brown state (p. 282):

> Lesbians are indeed a unique minority group. The minority status of lesbians is different from the minority status of heterosexual people of color and White non-lesbian women. First, discrimination against lesbians is both legal and socially sanctioned in this country. Such discrimination is no longer legal against people of color or White women, although social norms remain more resilient to change. Second, lesbianism, unlike skin color or gender, can often be hidden. Part of the heterosexism of our culture is that heterosexuality is assumed, and lesbianism and lesbians are generally invisible. Because a woman's lesbianism generally becomes known through her active disclosure of this information, lesbians usually have a choice about whether or not to be open at work.

In Friskopp and Silverstein's book, *Straight Jobs, Gay Lives* (1995), gay Harvard Business School alumni stated they felt they were about as successful as their straight classmates of the same race and sex, and minority and female gays reported much more discrimination based on their race, ethnicity, or sex than on their sexual orientation (Lewis, 1997). While the men often felt secure as they moved up, the women often felt less so—and retreated deeply into the closet (Swisher, 1996). As lesbians rise through the ranks of corporate America, some of them fear that the danger of disclosure rises with them (Swisher, 1996).

Lesbian Identity

Lesbians tend to demonstrate nontraditional sex roles. These nontraditional roles, combined with the expectation of being self-supporting through their lives, provide the motivation for lesbians to pursue male-dominated careers, which will likely be higher paying than traditionally woman-dominated careers (Chung, 1995). Lesbians' double minority status contributes to the complexities that they confront in life and career planning (Hetherington and Orzek, 1989). Lesbians often realize early in life that they will not marry, so they tend to invest more heavily in preparing for careers than straight women do (Black, Makar, Sanders, and Taylor, 2003).

Lesbians represent about 3.6 percent of the population (Degges-White and Shoffner, 2002) and according to the Federal Bureau of Investigation (quoted in Degges-White and Shoffner, 2002), hate crimes against lesbians increased between 1997 and 2002. Corporations, as microenvironments, must contend with this hatred. Therefore, lesbians in organizational America face a multiplicity of important considerations when managing their careers: occupational choice, lesbian identity development, and whether, to whom, where, and when to come out.

Vivienne Cass, an Australian psychotherapist, developed a model of homosexual identity development that may answer the question of why some gay people are content with themselves and others are quite unhappy (McNaught, 1993). A model of lesbian identity development is the Sophie model, which was developed in 1985 and tested through repeated structured interviews with fourteen women experiencing confusion about their sexual orientation (Fassinger, 1995). This model consists of four stages: (1) first awareness of homosexual feelings, (2) testing and exploration, (3) identity acceptance, and (4) identity integration. Understanding how these four stages work can assist in career development.

Advantages of Being a Lesbian in the Workplace

Lesbians have some advantages in the corporate world. For example, it has been noted that they tend to demonstrate more nontraditional, androgynous gender roles than heterosexual women do (Fassinger, 1996). Lesbian professionals who are openly gay are in the best position to reap the benefits of this stereotype. Friskopp and Silverstein (1995) tell the story of an openly gay woman who observed that people viewed her as a dedicated, appropriately aggressive professional who commanded the respect of men.

Lesbians, in comparison to heterosexual women, are less likely to make vocational and life choices based on accommodating men or conforming to traditional gender roles (Fassinger, 1996). Another aspect of lesbian identity that is likely to exert positive influence on career choice is that lesbians, in contrast to many of their heterosexual counterparts, do not expect to rely on men for financial support; they also tend to be more financially independent in their relationships, perhaps in part because legal restrictions largely prevent dependence in lesbian and gay relationships (Morgan and Brown, 1991). Thus, lesbians may be consciously or unconsciously planning at an

New Directions for Adult and Continuing Education • DOI: 10.1002/ace

early age for the eventuality of a career; an employment rate of about 90 percent among lesbians supports this assumption (Morgan and Brown, 1991).

In research conducted with heterosexual, gay, and lesbian college students, lesbians showed the least amount of uncertainty about their career decision making (Hetherington and Orzek, 1989), and lesbians and heterosexual men were the most satisfied with their career choices. An awareness of the need to support themselves, as well as the frequent devaluation of traditionally female jobs in the lesbian community (Morgan and Brown, 1991), may further encourage lesbians to consider nontraditional, and usually more highly paid, careers (Fassinger, 1995). Lesbians are unusually successful in gaining employment in largely male-dominated and better-remunerated occupational categories (Blandford, 2003).

Clearly, such fluidity of expectation allows lesbians to make freer and less constricted choices in their careers. Moreover, out lesbians are less threatening to men in the workplace because of the reduced sexual pressure or tension between the two parties. Lesbians are seen as being aggressive, nonemotional, tough, and reliable, which are qualities needed for management (Friskopp and Silverstein, 1995).

Fassinger (1995) has pointed out that despite a number of vocational barriers that lesbians may face, there are also important facilitative aspects of lesbian identity related to career planning and choice. Most salient among these is that lesbians tend to demonstrate more nontraditional, androgynous gender roles than do heterosexual women (Fassinger, 1996; Hetherington and Orzek, 1989; Morgan and Brown, 1991). Moreover, because lesbianism is difficult to physically distinguish, lesbians have the ability to hide their identities when their safety or security is threatened. Lesbian invisibility therefore is a two-edged sword. On one hand, this invisibility works to enable the homophobic, heterosexist, and sexist status quo of organizations. On the other hand, invisibility permits lesbians to make choices about their vulnerability. Lesbians must adroitly manage their identities with coworkers, supervisors, and clients when they choose to be open about their orientation, because of several factors that impinge on this decision. The effects of nonconformity often benefit lesbians, who not only gravitate toward male-dominated occupations but also succeed in managing the sexual politics and harassment that typify these types of work environments (Blandford, 2003).

Lesbians therefore experience a complex set of challenges as well as opportunities. The absence of research and practice that could provide training, development, and educational opportunities for lesbians does not mean that they have not learned how to succeed.

Lesbians and Learning

Lesbians in corporate America have learned the significance of their skill, ability, and willingness to prescreen, come out, and educate others on issues related to being lesbian. In her study of lesbian executives, managers, and directors in primarily Fortune 500 corporations, Gedro (2000) examined what lesbians learned about success and how they learned it. Lesbians have learned that it is important, when meeting a new person or new group of people, or entering a new organization, to prescreen for clues that indicate the person or group's receptivity toward the subject of lesbianism. The prescreen includes paying attention to visual clues such as religious symbols that might indicate a predilection for negative views toward homosexuality as well as verbal clues such as a stated or implied dislike for concepts, viewpoints, or orientations that are somehow perceived as different from their own. Second, lesbians in corporate America have learned that it is important to come out, and they have learned through their experience that while coming out is sometimes a daunting process, it most often has a positive result. Finally, lesbians in corporate America have learned that it is important not only to come out as individuals but to educate others about issues related to being lesbian in order to raise the awareness of their straight subordinates, peers, and supervisors.

Lesbians do not learn about success as lesbians through taking classes, reading books, or attending seminars; such programs do not exist. Rather, they learn informally and incidentally. Informal learning is learning through means that are not structured and prearranged, that is, not institutionally sponsored (Watkins and Marsick, 1992). Informal learning includes trial-and-error learning, mentoring, and coaching. Incidental learning happens as a by-product of another activity (Watkins and Marsick, 1992). Informal learning is characterized by learner intent, whereas incidental learning happens generally spontaneously and occurs after the learner has reflected on and processed the meaning of an experience.

Creating Inclusive Environments for Lesbians

The invisibility of lesbians in organizational settings perpetuates the problems they face. The lack of research, theory, and practice into ways of disrupting the double discrimination arising from heterosexism, homophobia, and sexism guarantees that lesbians continue to be challenged in their careers. The dearth of scholarly and practical exploration into the double bind that lesbians face invites adult education and HRD scholars to address these issues in order to create some formal knowledge around lesbian issues and, more important, begin to arrange some institutional, group, and individual offerings for education, intervention and empowerment.

Organizational-Level Interventions. The informal and incidental learning that lesbians acquire suggests several formal and intentional institutional activities and arrangements that could disrupt the heterosexism and sexism that lesbians face. At the organizational level, the heterosexism and sexism of an organization oppresses all lesbians. However, it is beyond the scope of one chapter to explore precise organizational cultures in order to assemble specific proposals for creating lesbian-affirming environments. According to Griffith and Hebl (2002), diversity training needs to specifically address issues of sexual orientation, and management "might consider greater attempts to educate workers specifically about gay/lesbian issues, foster a climate of acceptance, and articulate policies that clearly indicate that discrimination will not be tolerated, particularly because coworker reactions are so important to gay/lesbian employees' job satisfaction and job anxiety" (p. 1198).

Adult and Higher Education. Both managers and human resource managers would benefit from education about the oppressive effects of homophobia, heterosexism, and sexism on lesbians so that they can more confidently and more effectively work to support their lesbian employees, but also so that they can identify and disrupt covert and overt discriminatory practices. Many human resource managers ignore the issues that gays and lesbians face because they lack education about such issues (Lucas and Kaplan, 1994). The lack of education among managers serves to reinforce existing feelings and systems of oppression, as lesbian employees "expend significant energy managing their sexual orientation on the job, attempting to control whether, when, and to whom their orientation is disclosed" (Schneider, 1982; Woods, quoted in Blandford, 2003, p. 625).

Although the adult education, HRD, and business curriculum are poised to educate existing and future organizational leaders to "reject the hierarchies of abjection" (Warner, quoted in Carlin and DiGrazia, 2004, p. 773) of lesbian, gay, bisexual, and transgendered (LGBT) employees, they generally remain silent on these issues. McQuarrie (1998) offered three reasons that sexual orientation is missing in management curriculums: there is a lack of visible or physical distinction of LGBT people, issues of LGBT people go unidentified and unaddressed because of the invisibility of LGBTs, and the discussion of sexual orientation may pose a threat to instructors. Instructors who are gay or lesbian may fear that teaching about sexual orientation may require them to disclose their own sexual orientation, even if they are uncomfortable in doing so or worried that such disclosure may affect their jobs or careers (McQuarrie, 1998).

Instead of serving to disrupt pervasive societal heterosexism, the silence and invisibility of LGBT issues in adult education and in the business curriculum reinforce its stigmatization. Adult educators and faculty in higher education, and particularly those in business, can advance the cause of the fight for LGBT equality by locating sources that provide insights about LGBT employees and including discussions about LGBT issues in the business classroom and adult education settings. Allies of the advancement of the equal rights of LGBT people should strive to include LGBT issues in their courses. In addition, faculty and adult educators who are LGBT have the opportunity to serve as activists inside the classroom by coming out. By claiming space, voice, and presence, LGBT adult educators, HRD practitioners, business faculty, and allies are uniquely positioned to foster learning environments in which learners can be exposed to issues unique to lesbians that might otherwise be ignored.

Role Models. Exposure to role models has been noted as an important factor in career choice (Hetherington and Orzek, 1989). The lack of career role models for lesbians is the result of the double bind that lesbians face, yet the presence of role models could be a critical factor in untangling lesbians from this bind. Girls and women in the early stages of lesbian identity have limited exposure to role models who would assist in the career development process (Hetherington and Orzek, 1989). The literature on career development consistently reflects the lack of role models as negatively affecting career development, particularly of lesbians (Fassinger, 1995). Because lesbians generally remain closeted at work, they cannot serve as role models for other lesbians (Fassinger, 1995), which reinforces the trial-and-error learning identified and discussed by Gedro, Cervero, and Johnson-Bailey (2004). The elimination of organizational homophobia, heterosexism, and sexism could create encouragement for lesbians in positions of power and influence to come out of the closet so that they could serve as role models for younger lesbians. Occupational stereotyping serves as a barrier to lesbians' career planning and choice, and lesbians often avoid certain occupations that are associated with lesbianism (Hetherington and Orzek, 1989).

Implications for Research and Development. Instead of lesbians having to serve individually as change agents of heterosexuals' sensitivity and awareness of issues related to being lesbian, adult educators and HRD researchers and practitioners have an opportunity to close the gap. Several research opportunities would extend understanding about lesbians in organization settings, including examining lesbians who have not succeeded in the corporate environment, lesbians who remain closeted as a singular strategy of negotiating the heterosexism of the corporate setting, mentoring choices and mentoring relationships for lesbians, and development training and development opportunities that address the unique learning needs of lesbians.

Conclusion

Lesbians have to concurrently negotiate heterosexism, sexism, homophobia, and their own sexual identity development while establishing and cultivating their careers. Adult education and HRD are disciplines that are positioned to collect and institutionalize some wisdom and some strategies for interrupting oppressive power structures as well as to empower lesbians. The interruptions can happen in a variety of locations: at the organizational level, in the business curriculum, in management, and for lesbians themselves.

References

Alderson, K. "The Corporate Closet: Career Challenges of Gay and Lesbian Individuals." Paper presented at the Annual National Consultation on Career Development Convention, Ottawa, Ontario, Jan. 20–23, 2003.

Bierema, L. "A Feminist Approach to HRD Research." *Human Resource Development Quarterly*, 2002, 1(2), 244–268.

Black, D., Makar, H., Sanders, S., and Taylor, L. "The Earnings Effects of Sexual Orientation." *Industrial and Labor Relations Review,* 2003, *56*(3), 449–469.

Blandford, J. "The Nexus of Sexual Orientation and Gender in the Determination of Earnings." *Industrial and Labor Relations Review,* 2003, *56*(4), 622–643.

Boatwright, K. J., Gilbert, M. S., Forrest, L., and Ketzenberger, K. "Impact of Identity Development upon Career Trajectory: Listening to the Voices of Lesbian Women." *Journal of Vocational Behavior,* 1996, *48,* 210–228.

Button, S. "Identity Management Strategies Utilized by Lesbian and Gay Employees." *Group and Organization Management,* 2004, *29*(4), 470–494.

Carlin, D., and DeGrazia, J. (eds.). *Queer Cultures.* Upper Saddle River, N.J.: Pearson Prentice Hall, 2004.

Chung, B. "Career Decision Making of Lesbian, Gay, and Bisexual Individuals." *Career Development Quarterly,* 1995, *44*(2), 178–191.

Chung, B. "Work Discrimination and Coping Strategies: Conceptual Frameworks for Counseling Lesbian, Gay, and Bisexual Clients." *Career Development Quarterly,* 2001, *50,* 33–44.

Day, N. E., and Schoenrade, P. "Staying in the Closet Versus Coming Out: Relationships Between Communication About Sexual Orientation and Work Attitudes." *Personnel Psychology,* 1997, *50,* 147–163.

Degges-White, S., and Shoffner, M. "Career Counseling with Lesbian Clients: Using the Theory of Work Adjustment as a Framework." *Career Development Quarterly,* 2002, *51,* 87–96.

Fassinger, R. "From Invisibility to Integration: Lesbian Identity in the Workplace." *Career Development Quarterly,* 1995, *44*(2), 148–168.

Fassinger, R. "Notes from the Margins: Integrating Lesbian Experience into the Vocational Psychology of Women." *Journal of Vocational Behavior,* 1996, *48,* 160–175.

Friskopp, A., and Silverstein, S. *Straight Jobs, Gay Lives.* New York: Scribner, 1995.

Gedro, J. "Urban Cowgirls: How Lesbians Have Learned to Negotiate the Heterosexism of Corporate America." Unpublished doctoral dissertation, University of Georgia, 2000.

Gedro, J., Cervero, R., and Johnson-Bailey, J. "How Lesbians Learn to Negotiate the Heterosexism of Corporate America." *Human Resource Development International,* 2004, *7*(2), 181–195.

Griffin, P. *Strong Women, Deep Closets.* Champaign, Ill.: Human Kinetics, 1998.

Griffith, K., and Hebl, M. "The Disclosure Dilemma for Gay Men and Lesbians: 'Coming Out' at Work." *Journal of Applied Psychology,* 2002, *87*(6), 1191–1199.

Heldke, L., and O'Connor, P. (eds.). *Oppression, Privilege, and Resistance.* New York: McGraw-Hill, 2004.

Hetherington, C., and Orzek, A. "Career Counseling and Life Planning with Women." *Journal of Counseling and Development,* 1989, *68,* 52–57.

Levine, M., and Leonard, R. "Discrimination Against Lesbians in the Workplace." *Signs,* 1984, *9*(4), 700–710.

Lewis, G. "Straight Jobs, Gay Lives: Gay and Lesbian Professionals, the Harvard Business School, and the American Workplace: Straight Talk About Gays in the Workplace: Creating an Inclusive, Productive Environment for Everyone in Your Organization; and Others." *American Review of Public Administration,* 1997, *27*(1), 96–99.

Lucas, J., and Kaplan, M. "Unlocking the Corporate Closet." *Training and Development,* Jan. 1994, 35–38.

McNaught, B. *Gay Issues in the Workplace.* New York: St. Martin's Press, 1993.

McQuarrie, F. "Expanding the Concept of Diversity: Discussing Sexual Orientation in the Management Classroom." *Journal of Management Education,* 1998, *22*(2), 162–172.

Miller, D. *Freedom to Differ.* New York: New York University Press, 1998.

Morgan, K. S., and Brown, L. S. "Lesbian Career Development, Work Behavior, and Vocational Counseling." *Counseling Psychologist,* 1991, *19,* 273–291.

Niesche, R. "Power and Homosexuality in the Teaching Workplace." *Social Alternatives,* 2003, *22*(2), 43–46.

Ragins, B., Cornwell, J., and Miller, J. "Heterosexism in the Workplace." *Group and Organization Management,* 2003, *28*(1), 45–74.

Schneider, B. "Consciousness About Sexual Harassment Among Heterosexual and Lesbian Women Workers." *Journal of Social Issues,* 1982, *38,* 75–78.

Swisher, K. "Coming Out in Corporate America." *Working Woman,* 1996, *21,* 50–53.

Watkins, K. E., and Marsick, V. J. "Towards a Theory of Informal and Incidental Learning in Organizations." *International Journal of Lifelong Education,* 1992, *11,* 287–300.

JULIE GEDRO is an assistant professor of business, management, and economics at SUNY Empire State College in Syracuse, New York.

New Directions for Adult and Continuing Education • DOI: 10.1002/ace

5

This chapter examines changes in preservice and continuing teacher professional development that are aimed at addressing sexual minority issues in schools as students' learning places and teachers' workplaces.

The Quest for a Queer Inclusive Cultural Ethics: Setting Directions for Teachers' Preservice and Continuing Professional Development

André P. Grace, Kristopher Wells

Historically, sexual minority (lesbian, gay, bisexual, intersexual, transidentified, two-spirited,[1] and queer) teachers have been marginalized in Canadian education, culture, and society. While this chapter addresses the specifics of this marginalization in Canada and efforts to address it in law, legislation, and educational policy and practice, the discussion is relevant across many democratic contexts where sexual minority rights have been on national agendas in education and culture. A goal of this chapter is to contribute to our global understanding of sexual minority issues by allowing readers to compare what is unfolding in Canada to their own national contexts.

Although marginalization in the Canadian context is being countered significantly, this exclusion is still evident. For example, in its 1998 *Report on Education in Canada,* the Council of Ministers of Education, Canada (CMEC), arguably the country's national voice for education, failed to provide any focus on sexual minority teachers in discussions of both teacher training and development and targeted programs for specific at-risk groups. Yet the CMEC maintained, "Education reflects and influences the social, economic, political, and cultural changes happening around it" (p. 3). With these words, the CMEC demonstrated a distance from, if not ignorance regarding, what had been happening in Canadian legal and legislative arenas regarding sexual minority rights. In another example, the Surrey Teach-

NEW DIRECTIONS FOR ADULT AND CONTINUING EDUCATION, no. 112, Winter 2006 © 2006 Wiley Periodicals, Inc.
Published online in Wiley InterScience (www.interscience.wiley.com) • DOI: 10.1002/ace.236

ers' Association, British Columbia, in 2000 unequivocally stated that "schools remain one of the last bastions of tolerated hatred toward glbt [gay, lesbian, bisexual, and trans-identified] people" (p. 2). Although the teachers' association noted how important it is to care for all students and families, it did not mention how important it is to address tolerated hatred of sexual minority teachers and care for all teachers.

When teachers' associations fail to focus on sexual minority teachers, they are being oblivious to the tremendous pressure these disenfranchised professionals experience as they try to balance work (being a secure and productive teacher) with life (being a safe and content person). They are also failing to accept responsibility for what happens to these association members. Teachers' associations, along with all other sectors of education, including school administrations and staff, school district management, school trustees, and provincial and territorial departments of education, have an obligation to eradicate tolerated hatred toward sexual minority students and teachers in school settings. This obligation is clearly mandated by Section 15 of the Canadian Charter of Rights and Freedoms, which provides sexual minority citizens with constitutional protection against discrimination on the ground of sexual orientation (MacDougall, 2000). Section 15 calls on education and other institutions to move away from the exclusionary tradition of replicating silence and invisibility.

Nevertheless, in Canadian education, sexual minority students and teachers remain in a paradoxical struggle to be cared about in a caring profession (Grace and Wells, 2004). The perennial disenfranchisement of sexual minority students and teachers in school settings replicates the historical sociocultural positioning of these individuals as sex, sexual, and gender deviants. Stories of the risks, stereotyping, and marginalization that sexual minority teachers have faced are well documented (Canadian Teachers' Federation, and the Elementary Teachers' Federation of Ontario, 2002; Grace, 2002–2003). As well, stories of the symbolic and physical violence that sexual minority youth have sustained are well detailed in narratives about confusion, depression, substance abuse, alienation, truancy, quitting school, gay bashing, running away, and suicide (Grace and Wells, 2001; Ryan and Futterman, 1998). Increasingly, though, stories of at-risk, sexual minority youth are being transgressed by stories of those sexual minority youth who take up roles as social activists, cultural workers, and survivors (Grace and Wells, 2005; Friend, 1998). Similarly, some sexual minority teachers are organizing and taking on roles as advocates (Gay and Lesbian Educators of British Columbia, 2004).

In performing these roles, sexual minority students and teachers are resisting, deconstructing, and transforming their fugitive identity constructions so that they can fully be, become, and belong in schools and other sociocultural settings. Thus, beyond the concerns, fears, and even moral apprehensions that various educational interest groups may have, it is becoming quite clear that queer or gay is not going to go away and that Canadian education has to become more responsive and responsible in meeting the needs of sexual minorities and protecting them from bias, prejudice, discrimination, and other forms of violence. This includes both building and sharing knowledge and resources about sexual minorities. The Canadian Teachers' Federation and the Elementary Teachers' Federation of Ontario (2002) have advocated for and demonstrated such building and sharing in their landmark publication *Seeing the Rainbow,* in which they stress the need for all educational interest groups to have current and relevant information about sexual minority realities. This is crucial to counter ignorance, which often leads to fear and misunderstanding and even violence. This fact is well documented by Janoff (2005) in *Pink Blood: Homophobic Violence in Canada,* his book documenting the history of violence toward sexual minority Canadians and immigrants.

From these perspectives, we describe in this chapter representative progress in Canadian law and legislation that is now having a domino effect with respect to the development of inclusive educational policy and practice. We then explore why school culture lags behind despite this progress. Next, in seeking to confront this cultural dissonance, we survey our own initiatives in which we engage in professional action planning to engender social change and transformation of school culture. We conclude by accenting the need for this emergent work to continue.

Representative Progress in Canadian Law, Legislation, and Educational Policy

The Canadian Charter of Rights and Freedoms was entrenched in the Canadian Constitution in 1982. In 1985 Section 15 of the charter protecting individuals against discrimination came into effect. Since then, Canadian courts have upheld the charter and protected the individual rights of Canadians. While protection against discrimination on the ground of sexual orientation has arguably been provided since 1985, the Supreme Court of Canada clearly confirmed sexual orientation as an analogous ground to other personal characteristics in 1995 in *Egan and Nesbit* v. *Canada.* Since this influential decision, there has been a flurry of federal and provincial and territorial legislation and legal decisions that have addressed numerous welfare and work issues of sexual minority Canadians.

One of the most crucial Supreme Court of Canada decisions advancing sexual minority rights is the decision in *Vriend* v. *Alberta,* which confirmed equality rights for lesbian and gay Canadians (MacDougall, 2000). Delwin Vriend, an educator at Kings College, Edmonton, Alberta, had been dismissed in 1991 on the pretext that his employment violated that conservative institution's religious policy. The Supreme Court handed down its long-awaited decision in *Vriend* on April 2, 1998. The decision was in the educator's favor in his legal challenge to have sexual orientation read into the Alberta Individual Rights Protection Act. In its judgment, the Supreme Court deemed that act unconstitutional.

Vriend ultimately had repercussions for Alberta and other Canadian provinces and territories that had not yet moved on their own to extend provincial and territorial human rights legislation to prohibit discrimination against lesbians and gays. Overall, though, *Vriend* has had a much larger impact, albeit one accompanied by cultural discomfort and conservative resistance. It has challenged Canadian people and institutions to rethink a social, cultural, educational, and historical mind-set that has excluded or erased fellow citizens because their ways of being and loving do not fit within the confines of a heteronormative society. As well, it has provided them cause to reflect on their attitudes, values, beliefs, and actions in relation to sexual minorities whom the Supreme Court of Canada has accorded the right to live and work free from discrimination in safe and secure surroundings.

In the light of the prevalent and pervasive focus on legal and legislative changes aimed at respecting sexual minority individual rights, Canadian education is being asked, and is indeed required to respond, to acknowledge and accommodate sex, sexual, and gender differences in educational policy and practice. The need for such policy and practice focused on nondiscrimination that contributes safety, security, rights, and benefits for sexual minorities cannot be overemphasized (Zemsky and Sanlo, 2005). The Alberta Teachers' Association (ATA) is proving to be a leader in meeting this need (Wells, 2005). Following the *Vriend* decision in 1998, the ATA moved quickly to protect sexual minority students, passing a resolution at its 1999 annual representative assembly (ARA) to include sexual orientation as a category protected against discrimination in its Code of Professional Conduct. At its 2000 ARA, ATA members provided the same protection to sexual minority teachers by voting to include sexual orientation as a category of persons protected by equality provisions in its Declaration of Rights and Responsibilities for Teachers. At its 2003 ARA, the ATA became the first teachers' association in Canada to include gender identity in its Code of Professional Conduct, thus protecting transidentified students. In 2004 the ATA provided the same protection to transidentified teachers. In 2005 the ATA passed a resolution to enable and support the establishment of gay-straight student alliance groups in Alberta high schools (Wells, 2005). Our national research indicates this progress in inclusive educational policymaking is also evident in the efforts of other provincial and territorial teachers' associations. At least at this level in education, progress is being made to include sexual minorities in policy and practice.

Why School Culture Lags Behind

Post-1982 legal and legislative changes in Canada and ensuing moves in inclusive educational policymaking have nevertheless not translated into full access and accommodation for sexual minority students and teachers. Although these changes have laid a basis for increased protection of sexual minorities in schools, culture, and society, transformation of Canadian education to make space and place for sexual minorities remains a slow, incremental process. Sexual minority students and teachers still confront heterosexism, transphobia, and homophobia daily in the generally conservative climate and culture of schools. Since support for sexual minority rights in Canada coexists with still evident disapproval of sexual minority citizens on political and moral grounds, sexual minority students and teachers are often left stranded in the sociocultural life of schools. Indeed, there has been a profound silencing of homosexuality in Canadian classrooms (MacDougall, 2000) despite charter protection.

Nevertheless, it is expected—indeed, mandated—that those involved in Canadian education engage in a public ethical practice that protects and respects the diversity of every student and teacher across differences of race, national or ethnic origin, color, religion, sex, age, mental or physical disability, and sexual orientation. Yet when it comes to sexual minority students and teachers, gay taunts and gay bullying are often ignored or dismissed. Indeed there remains a significant distance between education policy development and its full implementation in school life when it comes to sexual minority students and teachers. There are several reasons that this is the case. First, inclusive performativity based on a queer inclusive cultural ethics is often impeded by a politics of fear and caution in which educational interest groups placate conservative parents, religious leaders, politicians, and community groups that would eradicate everything queer from schools in an effort to maintain heteronormative tradition and the status quo. Often principals, teachers, and other educational interest groups fear these conservatives will target them for retribution. This everyday politics exacerbates anti-queerness—denouncing and dismissing queer ways of being, believing, desiring, becoming, belonging, and acting—in everyday language use, representations, and practices.

Second, in the context of schooling, sexual minority students have learned that they must be change agents of their own liberation because many teachers and school administrators, including closeted and fearful sexual minority professionals, tend not to support them (Harris Interactive and GLSEN, 2005). These educators fail to respond for various reasons (Grace and Wells, 2005; Human Rights Watch, 2001; King and Brindley, 2002):

They are part of the school's sexual minority population, and they fear the repercussions of being out and visible in their workplaces. They could also fear becoming role models for sexual minority students because of those in society who would conflate this role with being a recruiter to some misconstrued queer cause.

They are heterosexual allies, but they are afraid of being perceived as non-heterosexual.

New Directions for Adult and Continuing Education • DOI: 10.1002/ace

They lack the training needed to handle issues related to sexual orientation and gender identity.

They blame sexual minority students for being too vocal and visible about their sex, sexual, and gender differences.

They let personal moral beliefs interfere with their professional responsibility to engage in a public ethical practice that meets the needs of sexual minority students.

They are homophobic and perpetrators themselves, actively targeting sexual minority youth.

For these and other reasons, sexual minority students observe that the most common response of teachers and school administrators to the injustices they suffer is no response (Human Rights Watch, 2001).

Third, the vast majority of sexual minority students and teachers emphatically state that they view school administrators and parents as the primary barriers when it comes to attending to sex, sexual, and gender differences in education (Harris Interactive and GLSEN, 2005; Grace and Wells, 2005; Ryan and Futterman, 1998; Wells, 2002, 2003). This dynamic accentuates the need for educational policies that (1) protect sexual minority students (personally and as learners and minors in schools) and teachers (personally and as professionals employed in schools as teachers' workplaces), (2) ensure support mechanisms for sexual minority students and teachers in crisis, and (3) support cultural education about sex, sexual, and gender differences for all educational interest groups (Surrey Teachers' Association, 2000; Grace, 2002–2003; Wells, 2002. This educational work has been hampered historically by ignorance, fear, and the kind of private morality that is determined to preempt public ethical and inclusive educational work to respect and accommodate sexual minorities (Grace, Hill, Johnson, and Lewis, 2004).

Professional Action Planning to Engender Social Change and Transformation of School Culture

To confront school culture and the larger culture when they leave sexual minorities out, we engage in preservice and continuing professional development with teachers and other educational interest groups to help counter the politics of fear and caution that limits inclusion. This work is about building queer knowledge and understanding, and it is focused on "advocacy for empowerment and development of voice" (Hill, 2004, p. 87). We do this work in our university and with the Alberta Teachers' Association to help teachers and their co-interest groups become responsive and responsible in the work to create inclusive educational environments for sexual minorities.

In planning and implementing professional development action plans, we gauge inclusive performativity as cultural work for queer justice that addresses issues of personal safety, professional security, and access and accommodation in schools. This work is part of our ambition to have educational interest groups live out a queer inclusive cultural ethics enabling voice and visibility in schools. It focuses on identifying and addressing the challenges, risks, liabilities, and possibilities that can mark efforts to recognize, respect, and accommodate students and teachers across sex, sexual, and gender differences. Since this work takes educational interest groups into the still dangerous intersection of the moral and the political, it also focuses on identified needs that institutionalized education ought to meet if efforts aimed at sexual minority inclusion are to be successful.

Agape. As gay men and educators of educators, we feel obligated to assist sexual minority students and teachers and their allies in sociocultural and political work aimed at experienced inclusion. In our university context, we engage in this work through Agape, our faculty of education focus group that provides a forum for students, faculty, staff, and community members to take up issues of sex, sexual, and gender differences in education and culture. Agape, as Martin Luther King Jr. understood it, stands for "disinterested love. . . . Agape does not begin by discriminating between worthy and unworthy people, or any qualities people possess. It begins by loving others for their sakes. . . . It springs from the need of the other person" (cited in Tierney, 1993, p. 23). From this inclusive perspective, our group is designed to focus on the personal and professional needs that sexual minority undergraduate and graduate students, faculty, and staff have. Allies are also welcome. In addition, we reach out to the greater Edmonton community, inviting teachers working in K–12 schools and other interested community members to participate with us.

Agape members have worked to build an on-campus sexual minority resource base that is available to preservice and practicing teachers and community members. In our monthly meetings, we variously:

- Share and discuss narratives of schooling
- Use forms of sexual minority popular culture, including queer-themed music, films, and magazines, as resources to help us build teaching practices that counter heterosexism and homophobia
- Take up issues in relation to job searches and schools as teachers' workplaces
- Engage in role plays and other forms of drama as pedagogy to explore sexual minority issues and concerns in relation to schooling
- Examine policies and practices in schools, districts, and provincial teachers' associations across Canada
- Examine materials from various safe and caring schools' initiatives and coalitions in Canada and the United States
- Deliberate with invited presenters including sexual minority researchers and activists as well as community groups like PFLAG (Parents, Families, and Friends of Lesbians and Gays)
- Provide a space to network and socialize in a safe, supportive setting

As well, each autumn Agape members host a conference using the theme of sex, sexual, and gender differences in education and culture. In November 2005, our fifth annual conference provided an opportunity for educational interest groups from local, provincial, and national jurisdictions to come together to engage in dialogue and share knowledge and resources. Featured speakers included an out gay vice president of the Canadian Teachers' Federation, a school superintendent involved in advancing sexual minority–inclusive education in his district, and a former president of the Alberta Teachers' Association who was instrumental in early initiatives to develop sexual minority–inclusive policies. The conference provided everyone present with an opportunity to assess changes, progress, and possibilities regarding the inclusion of sexual minority students and teachers in schools.

Preservice Teacher Education. Through Agape, we engage in other initiatives with preservice teachers, cognizant that education remains a conservative space—a space that tends to tolerate or assimilate difference, when difference is attended to at all, rather than to let difference be or to respect and accommodate it. For example, each term we give workshops for all preservice teachers registered in Educational Policy Studies 310—Managing the Learning Environment, our core teaching methods course. We invite colleagues and members of PFLAG and other community groups to help us deliver these workshops to several hundred undergraduates a year. The workshops focus on addressing issues of sexual minority differences in school settings, building a resource base, and networking with the larger community. In addition to inviting guest speakers, we use videos, narrative vignettes and poetry, and resource handouts to focus discussions about sex, sexual, and gender differences; heterosexism; transphobia; homophobia; violence; and schooling. We include a discussion on guidelines for developing an inclusive curriculum and bias-free teaching materials. We also highlight initiatives, like the Society for Safe and Caring Schools and Communities, that operate to promote the educational interests of sexual minority and other students for whom schools can be unsafe places.

Continuing Professional Development with the Alberta Teachers' Association. If we consider teaching to be a vocation, then we must be there for every student. This is not an easy task since teachers and other educational interest groups are expected to uphold tradition and be transmitters of culture and preservers of the status quo. Sadly, elements of the dominant culture desiring to maintain the status quo variously exclude others on the basis of differences they find unacceptable. Perhaps the most morally and politically marginalized differences are sexual minority differences that lie outside male-female and heterosexual psychosocial norms. Teachers, called to engage in an ethical, respectful, and just educational practice, cannot ignore these differences. In this light, teachers need to know about and understand the parameters of sexual orientation and gender identity and expression. The Alberta Teachers' Association is providing its members with such an opportunity through a series of workshops that

New Directions for Adult and Continuing Education • DOI: 10.1002/ace

one of us (Kris) developed and the other of us (André) reviewed.

The series, entitled Building Safe, Caring, and Inclusive Schools for Lesbian, Gay, Bisexual and Transgender (LGBT) Students, is composed of three workshops intended to stimulate a critical dialogue that examines the attitudes and beliefs that teachers, students, the school, and the community hold about LGBT people. Workshop 1, Building Awareness of Sexual Orientation and Gender Identity Issues, helps teachers begin to build knowledge and understanding of the everyday lived experiences and safety and health concerns that many sexual minority students face in their classrooms, schools, and communities. Teachers also investigate the feelings that sexual minorities have regarding their safety, inclusion, health, and wellness in schools. Workshop 2, Exploring Diversity Issues Related to Sexual Orientation and Gender Identity, assists teachers to understand their professional, ethical, and legal responsibilities regarding the equitable and safe treatment of LGBT students. Teachers also learn to break down stereotypes and challenge binary thinking that can limit student expressions of individuality and difference. Workshop 3, Creating Safe and Caring Learning Environments for LGBT Students, enables teachers to explore specific strategies and resources that they can use to create safe, caring, and inclusive spaces for sexual minority students. Teachers use case studies to help them think about issues and concerns that sexual minority students and teachers face in school, classroom, and community contexts. Endorsing this workshop series, Fern Snart, dean of the Faculty of Education at the University of Alberta, has written (quoted in Wells, 2003, p. 1):

> The commitment of the Alberta Teachers' Association to support the learning needs of all students is reflected in these materials focusing on the needs of Lesbian, Gay, Bisexual and Transgender (LGBT) students. Workshops include insights into the challenges of LGBT students, and encourage dialogue and self-reflection. The prepared materials offer a refreshing opportunity to replace prejudice with knowledge and understanding, and they do so with candor and compassion. Congratulations to the developers for resources to move us closer to a place where misconceptions die, and wherein students are accepted as unique, talented individuals who are defined by their characters and contributions.

Conclusion

Progressive moves in Canadian law and legislation provide a framework to develop institutional supports and cultural practices enabling the acceptance and accommodation of sexual minority citizens in education and other sociocultural contexts. Nevertheless, in dispositional and practical terms, Canadian culture and society still lag behind the law and legislation in building the kind of inclusive spaces that legal judgments and legislative acts have guaranteed. Despite some progress in education, there remains a

New Directions for Adult and Continuing Education • DOI: 10.1002/ace

pressing need to focus on diversity, equity, welfare, and inclusion in relation to sexual minority students and teachers who need personal and professional supports. There is a pressing need as well to educate teachers, school administrators, and other educational interest groups, including parents, politicians, and church groups, regarding sex, sexual, and gender differences and the rights of sexual minority citizens with respect to these differences. Such community education is vital. It is part of building an inclusive ethical pedagogy and a just society. It is part of according sexual minority persons the rights and respect that every Canadian is due.

Note

1. *Two-spirited* is a term employed by Native Americans and First Nation peoples denoting that both masculine and feminine spirits live within some individuals, constituting a "third-gender" category.

References

Canadian Teachers' Federation, and the Elementary Teachers' Federation of Ontario (eds.). *Seeing the Rainbow: Teachers Talk About Bisexual, Gay, Lesbian, Transgender and Two-Spirited Realities.* Ottawa: Canadian Teachers' Federation, and the Elementary Teachers' Federation of Ontario, 2002.

Council of Ministers of Education, Canada. *Report on Education in Canada.* Toronto: Council of Ministers of Education, Canada, 1998.

Friend, R. A. "Heterosexism, Homophobia, and the Culture of Schooling." In S. Brooks (ed.), *Invisible Children in the Society and Its Schools.* Mahwah, N.J.: Erlbaum, 1998.

Gay and Lesbian Educators of British Columbia. *Challenging Homophobia in Schools.* (2nd ed.) Nelson Park, BC: Gay and Lesbian Educators of British Columbia, 2004.

Grace, A. P. "Breaking the Silence on LGBTQ Issues in Saskatchewan: An Interview with Don Cochrane." *Torquere: Journal of the Canadian Lesbian and Gay Studies Association,* 2002–2003, *4–5,* 202–212.

Grace, A. P., Hill, R. J., Johnson, C. W., and Lewis, J. B. "In Other Words: Queer Voices/Dissident Subjectivities Impelling Social Change." *International Journal of Qualitative Studies in Education,* 2004, *17*(3), 301–323.

Grace, A. P., and Wells, K. "Getting an Education in Edmonton, Alberta: The Case of Queer Youth." *Torquere, Journal of the Canadian Lesbian and Gay Studies Association,* 2001, *3,* 137–151.

Grace, A. P., and Wells, K. "Engaging Sex-and-Gender Differences: Educational and Cultural Change Initiatives in Alberta." In M. Cronin and J. McNinch (eds.), *I Could Not Speak My Heart: Education and Social Justice for Gay and Lesbian Youth.* Regina, SK: Canadian Plains Research Centre, 2004.

Grace, A. P., and Wells, K. "The Marc Hall Prom Predicament: Queer Individual Rights v. Institutional Church Rights in Canadian Public Education." *Canadian Journal of Education,* 2005, *28*(3), 237–270.

Harris Interactive and GLSEN. *From Teasing to Torment: School Climate in America: A Survey of Students and Teachers.* New York: Gay, Lesbian, and Straight Education Network, 2005.

Hill, R. J. "Activism as Practice: Some Queer Considerations." In R. St. Clair and J. A. Sandlin (eds.), *Promoting Critical Practice in Adult Education.* New Directions for Adult and Continuing Education, no. 102. San Francisco: Jossey-Bass, 2004.

Human Rights Watch. "Hatred in the Hallways: Violence and Discrimination against Lesbian, Gay, Bisexual, and Transgender Students in U.S. Schools." http://www.hrw. org/reports/2001/uslgbt. Accessed July 5, 2004.

Janoff, D. V. *Pink Blood: Homophobic Violence in Canada.* Toronto: University of Toronto Press, 2005.

King, J. R., and Brindley, R. "Teacher Educators and the Multicultural Closet: The Impact of Gay and Lesbian Content on an Undergraduate Teacher Education Seminar." In R. M. Kissen (ed.), *Getting Ready for Benjamin: Preparing Teachers for Sexual Diversity in the Classroom.* Lanham, Md.: Rowman and Littlefield, 2002.

MacDougall, B. *Queer Judgments: Homosexuality, Expression, and the Courts in Canada.* Toronto: University of Toronto Press, 2000.

Ryan, C., and Futterman, D. *Lesbian and Gay Youth: Care and Counseling.* New York: Columbia University Press, 1998.

Surrey Teachers' Association. *"Moving Beyond Silence": Addressing Homophobia in Elementary Schools.* Surrey, B.C.: Surrey Teachers' Association, 2000.

Tierney, W. G. *Building Communities of Difference.* Toronto: Ontario Institute for Studies in Education Press, 1993.

Wells, K. "Sexual Orientation and Gender Identity: A Professional Development Website for Alberta Teachers." 2002. http://www.teachers.ab.ca/Issues+In+Education/ Diversity+and+Human+Rights/Sexual+Orientation/Index.htm. Accessed Dec. 18, 2005.

Wells, K. *Building Safe, Caring, and Inclusive Classrooms, Schools, and Communities for Lesbian, Gay, Bisexual and Transgender Students: Professional Development Workshops for Alberta Teachers.* Edmonton: Alberta Teachers' Association, 2003.

Wells, K. *Gay–Straight Student Alliances in Alberta Schools: A Guide for Teachers.* Edmonton: Alberta Teachers' Association, 2005.

Zemsky, B., and Sanlo, R. L. "Do Policies Matter?" In R. L. Sanlo (ed.), *Gender Identity and Sexual Orientation: Research, Policy, and Personal Perspectives.* New Directions for Student Services, no. 111. San Francisco: Jossey-Bass, 2005.

ANDRÉ P. GRACE *is a professor in the Department of Educational Policy Studies, University of Alberta, Edmonton, Canada.*

KRISTOPHER WELLS *is a doctoral student and Canada Scholar in the Department of Educational Policy Studies, University of Alberta, Edmonton, Canada.*

6

This chapter explores the dilemmas and perceptions of being open regarding nonheterosexual sexual orientations in the higher education classroom from the individual perspectives of the three coauthors.

Difficult Dilemmas: The Meaning and Dynamics of Being Out in the Classroom

Thomas V. Bettinger, Rebecca Timmins, Elizabeth J. Tisdell

The decision about whether to be out as a lesbian, gay, bisexual, transgender, or queer (LGBTQ) person in a heterosexist society as well as in the higher education classroom is often a dilemma. It is usually dependent on a multitude of factors, including the context, whether direct discussion of sexual orientation seems relevant to the course, the political and institutional climate, one's relationship status, the degree to which one feels safe, one's emotional energy on a given day, and the nature of the relationship among those in the learning environment. A further complication is that coming out, that is, self-disclosing, is a never-ending process (Sedgwick, 1990). In each new situation, some people will not realize the sexual orientation of even the most out person. Thus, although one might be out to colleagues, friends, and family members, one almost invariably faces the dilemma of whether to be out when entering a new higher education classroom.

In this chapter, we explore how the three of us navigate these dilemmas in the higher education classroom in our own context at a university in the moderately conservative area of south-central Pennsylvania. One of us (Libby Tisdell) is a faculty member, and two of us (Thom Bettinger and Becky Timmins) are students in the adult education doctoral program and have served in teaching roles in higher education, in our own workplaces, and in community settings. Each of us discusses our own individual expe-

riences of how we deal with these dilemmas, and then we have a dialogue about issues related to being out in the classroom.

Our Individual Navigations

Libby's Perspective. I have been a full-time faculty member in higher education settings for the past thirteen years. How I have dealt with sexual orientation issues in the classroom is indeed dependent on the context of my own life, the institution in which I am teaching, the learners I am working with, and the course content. As a teacher, my concern about what to discuss, including what seems personal, is whether it facilitates students' learning. I teach a multitude of courses, but I have found that particularly in teaching diversity courses, ultimately it serves students' learning around sexual orientation if I am up front about my own.

My own sexual orientation cannot be easily categorized, and as a poststructural feminist, I believe all categorizations need to be problemetized. Yet if I had to define it, I would say that it is contextual. As I have discussed elsewhere (Tisdell, 2001), I fall in love with a person, not a gender. The context of that love relationship itself determines both my primary sexual and affectional orientation. Until I was thirty-one years old, I had lived entirely as heterosexual and never really questioned it, for, as Adrienne Rich notes (1980), heterosexuality appeared compulsory. I then fell head over heels in love with a woman. We became partners and stayed happily together for eleven years. During that time, I secured my first full-time academic position in a liberal part of the country in a liberal academic institution. There, after some experimentation with teaching and getting more comfortable with both my own role as a teacher as well as my own outness in this context, I discovered that discussing my own family life and sexual orientation typically engendered more openness in dealing with diversity issues in the classroom. Thus, I learned to get over my nervousness, and in the first class of diversity courses, I would discuss my life in a committed relationship with my female partner. People defined me as a lesbian, which was okay with me, though I never exactly classified myself as necessarily exclusively lesbian, or bisexual, or straight, since for me my sexual orientation is contextual, and related more to a person and a relationship, than with one gender or another.

Following the ending of that partnership in the late 1990s, for the usual reasons that couples split up (for example, growing to want different things, though not necessarily a partner of another gender), I moved twice and taught in two different universities. For several years, I was single and not dating seriously. Then about six years ago, I fell in love with a man with whom I am partnered and have a committed relationship. Although it may appear to others that I was confused before (or am now!) or have caved into the demands of "compulsory heterosexuality" and "gone straight," I have not changed my sexual orientation given that it is contextually situated as being in love with and committed to a particular person regardless of her or his gender.

New Directions for Adult and Continuing Education • DOI: 10.1002/ace

How I have navigated discussing sexual orientation issues in my classroom, including my own sexual orientation and history, has not changed particularly; it is dependent on the context and what facilitates student learning. I generally include some readings about sexual orientation related to the content of the course in all my classes. But I discuss my own sexual orientation and my related life experiences primarily in diversity and equity classes in relation to the complexity of systems of privilege and oppression including sexual orientation. I do it in this context for multiple reasons: there is time, it is directly relevant to the course content, and most students know me because I have taught them in a prior course and are generally open to both my teaching style and diversity issues in general due to exposure in prior classes. Although my sexual orientation is not a secret because I have written about and discussed it publicly, I discuss it directly in my classes when it is most relevant to the course content, to support LGBTQ students and faculty, and in my effort to facilitate all students' learning while attempting to teach for equity and justice.

Becky's Perspective. I never imagined the extent to which the adult education classroom would affect my life and create space for discussions regarding sexual orientation. My life has been entrenched in the sports world as a coach of women's basketball and a health educator. The sports world is engulfed in sexism, heterosexism, and homophobia, which produce silence, lesbian labels, and double identities for lesbians in sports (Griffin, 1998). The sports world has been a large part of my life since childhood. Collegiate coaching was a career that provided a continuation in the sports world; therefore, I developed a sense of myself in a heterosexist atmosphere. The combination of my passion for sports and the homophobic and heterosexist environment provided a difficult path, including a life of silence and a life of double identity (coach and lesbian) on campus, and I remained in the closet throughout my undergraduate and graduate years. Recently I had the opportunity to change careers and step out of the deeply discriminatory world of sports.

Upon changing careers, I also enrolled in an adult education doctoral program and became part of a cohort of sixteen students. I had not been in the classroom as a student for eight years and had never come out in the classroom setting. During these eight years, I had the opportunity to explore aspects of my identity. I had begun to navigate life as a committed person in a relationship and was in the midst of building a home and beginning a family with my significant other. As I started the journey with my cohort, LGBTQ issues in the political world were receiving considerable attention, largely due to the issue of same-sex marriage and the polarizing 2004 presidential campaign. My life as a lesbian seemed to be very much a public, socially scrutinizable construct (Yescavage and Alexander, 1997), yet I was unsure of what path I would take as an LGBTQ member of my cohort. Unbeknownst to me at the time, the energy and empowerment created by my personal life and my growing

New Directions for Adult and Continuing Education • DOI: 10.1002/ace

political awareness and involvement would set the stage for a sense of liberation in the classroom.

The first time our cohort met for class, discussions of children and spouses arose. I was not quite sure how I would explain my commitment ring on my left ring finger, as some of the students referred to my significant other as my "husband." I decided for the first time to be open and honest to those sensitive enough to ask. A month into the first semester, a class assignment surrounding diversity in the classroom prompted a discussion of equality and gay rights. As the group began to discuss their perspectives on gay rights, some expressed views that did not support or were dismissive of equal rights for sexual minorities. In response, I announced that I am gay and deserving of equal rights. Some comments from classmates included, "I've never met a homosexual before" and "I knew but was waiting for you to tell us."

I attribute the ability for me to come out to the safe classroom that my professor created, the discourse of a diverse classroom, the grounding of myself as a person, and my passion and need to share my lived experiences as a lesbian with my cohort. The inclusion of articles by and about LGBTQ people, the discussions of marginalized groups, and the open environment created by my professors enable a safe place to learn. This is the first time in my life that sexual orientation has been recognized and discussed openly in a formal educational setting. I feel empowered as I continue to engage in the literature surrounding LGBTQ people. I feel a sense of belonging in my cohort because I am comfortable discussing my experiences as a lesbian. The decision of my professors to address sexual orientation issues and the acceptance of my peers has created a safe place for me to be authentic. A growing sense of advocacy combined with the lack of research by lesbian adult educators has prompted me to follow my passion by pursuing research in this area. The sense of empowerment and belonging produced by my involvement in the adult education experience has been life changing.

Thom's Perspective. I would prefer that being out in the classroom would be taken for granted and no big deal. However, given the deeply ensconced heterosexism and homophobia in Western society, being an out graduate student, even in the field of adult education with its rich and long-standing history of social justice, can be a difficult dilemma. Hill (2004) believes that all education advocates something; that is, it defends or maintains a cause. This advocacy can be expressed in many ways, from silently reinforcing the status quo to promoting activism—"direct action contesting or upholding one side of a controversial issue" (p. 85). Activism can take many positions, ranging from engaging in education for social change to open protest and civil disobedience. My choice to be explicitly out is both an expression of activism and a political act, yet it is also a point of personal integrity and critical to my ongoing process of becoming grounded in my own authenticity rather than being who others said I should be, or what Abalos (1998) refers to as reclaiming one's sacred face.

New Directions for Adult and Continuing Education • DOI: 10.1002/ace

My decision to be out in the classroom was influenced by numerous factors, including the privilege accorded by my status as a white, middle-aged, and middle-class male. Multiply oppressed sexual minorities (for example, women, persons of color, and those who are disabled) may face additional and considerably more difficult dilemmas in deciding if and when coming out in the classroom is prudent. Yet privilege notwithstanding, my own experiences indicate what a complex decision and process this can be. I first came out, rather nonchalantly, in the classroom setting as an undergraduate in the mid-1970s. Given the liberal environment of a large university, this was basically a nonevent. Such was not the case several years later when, as a part-time graduate student at a smaller, rural college, I again came out in the classroom. In retrospect, I realize I was naive not to take the context (including the conservative area) into consideration. Thus, I was somewhat unprepared and nonplussed when I was treated with disdain by the professor, a situation that ultimately led to my decision to withdraw from the program.

While taking additional graduate courses in the late 1980s, I did not come out. Still stinging from a decade earlier, I concluded it was too risky given the environment of extreme societal homophobia and right-wing political and fundamentalist religious backlash toward gays that was exacerbated by the HIV/AIDS epidemic. I also did not come out during my master's program in the late 1990s. In this case, I simply was not willing to invest the emotional energy required to be out in the classroom setting; internalized homophobia and the perceived risk to my professional career were likely implicated as well. Nevertheless, I was torn by the illusory sense of safety and security gained at the cost of invisibility and silence of my true self. It is extremely taxing to compartmentalize one's life, that is, to be out in some contexts and closeted in others. I still wonder how much richer both my learning and my relationships with other students and professors might have been in those situations had I not used so much time and emotional energy on the "paralyzing demands of hiding" (Kissen, 1996, p. 3). Thus, when I entered the doctoral program, I realized I could not make such a commitment and keep my sexual orientation hidden. I was not exactly sure how I would go about self-disclosing. I would respond truthfully if asked, and if no one asked, I would bring it up when it seemed right. This approach provided me the opportunity to assess the environment and context and allowed time for me to feel comfortable.

It is almost a truism that educators' attitudes and actions have tremendous impact on learning environments and outcomes. This may especially be the case regarding LGBTQ students. Without the support and encouragement of faculty, the risks these students face might present too much of a barrier for some to overcome. An affirming faculty, regardless of their sexual orientation, has certainly made things easier for me than might otherwise have been the case. This is not to imply that being out in my adult education program has been carefree. In describing the lived reality of

New Directions for Adult and Continuing Education • DOI: 10.1002/ace

LGBTQ lives, Hill (2004) comments, "We have seen the consequences of being considered indecent, offensive, or anathema to public sentiments and socialization: marginalization and silencing at best, violence and death at worst" (p. 86). While these extremes may be unlikely in an academic setting, LGBTQ persons do risk being ostracized, or essentialized and thought of merely in terms of sexual orientation. Indeed, a cohort member once commented "I don't care what you do in bed," as if I, as a gay man, would be any more inclined to discuss intimate details of my life than would anyone else. Furthermore, due to the iterative nature of coming out, I have to continually assess each interaction as to what those involved already know about me and ascertain whether to disclose my status as a sexual minority. These are risks I have considered and am willing to undertake, for, like hooks (1994), I am coming to see silence as an act of complicity—in this case, reinforcing heteronormativity.

Being out in the classroom also has benefits that I have determined outweigh the risks for me. According to Tierney (1997), there will always be individuals in colleges and universities who are willing to support LGBTQ persons, but they often do not know how to do so. They are not homophobic; rather, they are simply fearful of intruding, or they think their help or advice may not be wanted. Being out in the program allows me to contest heterosexism and share my experiences so that others, particularly those who would be allies, might learn about the challenges sexual minorities face. I share because of the "need for critical thinkers to engage multiple locations, to address diverse standpoints, to allow us to gather knowledge fully and inclusively" (hooks, 1994, p. 91). It is a way of encouraging others to engage not only with the cognitive aspects of homophobia and heterosexism but with the affective components as well. In the process, my personal learning is deepened and more authentic. At times, being out also has afforded opportunities such as presentations or team teaching that I might not have had otherwise. Even more gratifying have been those times when others have approached me to discuss loved ones who were themselves struggling with sexual identity issues. Such instances, small as they may seem, serve as affirmation of my decision.

A Continuing Dialogue on Closets and Contexts

There are two central and interrelated themes that are apparent in our individual reflections that we reflected on together in our online and face-to-face discussions of these issues that are worthy of further discussion: the issue of context and the fluid nature of the closet, or what it means to be out. We share some of our reflections here:

THOM: What strikes me most is how each of us highlighted how critical context is to this whole issue and the intricacies and complexities that differing contexts within higher education can weave. Yet it seems that context is also used as a rationale to inhibit coming out in the classroom—and to me, this hinges largely on heterosexism. For instance, a standard argument is that sexual orientation has nothing to do with math or whatever other subject, so it is irrelevant in the math classroom. While I may have bought into that notion before entering the doctoral program, I now am more likely to see this argument as reinforcing heteronormativity (meaning that what is heterosexual is "normative" and thus seen as "acceptable"). Our sexual orientation or identity is part of who we are (even as it may shift) in every context, including in higher education. It has an impact on what we learn (teach), how we learn (teach), why we learn (teach), and what we do with the learning (teaching). So regardless of the subject matter, each of us brings that aspect of ourselves to the situation; as such, sexual identity is a site of learning for all of us, whether we realize it or not. Heteronormativity would have us believe it does not matter, and therefore we should remain silenced; meanwhile, heterosexism is operating as usual, and those who are heterosexual are free to be their true selves, while those of us who are not are expected to shut off that aspect of ourselves.

LIBBY: Thom, that's really an excellent point. On one level, it is always related to learning and to the more authentic identity of teacher and learner. But I am going to play devil's advocate here. Other aspects that affect learning are as central to who one is as one's sexual orientation. One such example is one's spiritual view of the world. As one who has actually taught math in the college classroom, I was as equally unlikely to refer to my sexual orientation or female partner as I was to my spirituality in that context, because it was not very obviously relevant to the course content. That is not to discount your contention that not discussing sexual orientation tends to reinforce heteronormativity since people are often presumed to be heterosexual unless otherwise stated.

BECKY: This issue of context reminds me of cohort discussions regarding the relevance of sexual orientation to adult education. We bring our experiences into the adult education classroom as a source of learning. My lens is that of a lesbian student, and if I cannot feel free to bring my life experiences to the classroom, then I cannot be authentic, which ultimately decreases learning opportunities for me as well as others. For years, I used an extraordinary amount of energy to separate my personal life from my profession and my education. Now the safe classroom environment enables me to connect with my own experiences, and the openness allows my cohort to discuss sexual minority topics.

THOM: That relevance issue is commonly posed to those who are out in education, but if one stops and thinks about it, the question is really very heterosexist in that the one asking it is usually (although not always) heterosexual and would not be ill disposed to mentioning her or his spouse or other social markers to which we are excluded. The question exemplifies the notion of hypervisibility; that is, heterosexuals are free to be themselves, but the mere mention or indication of one's nonheterosexual status leads to accusations of "flaunting it."

LIBBY: So what do you think of not coming out in the classroom, either as a teacher or as a student when the opportunity presents itself, if one has more or less been out in similar contexts?

BECKY: I feel that lack of discussion surrounding sexual minorities is a direct result of internalized homophobia and is perpetuated by the fear and backlash of coming out. As I continue to come out, communicate my feelings, or interact in social situations, my own internalized homophobia surfaces— even as subtle as neglecting to rebut a comment when someone responds negatively about sexual minorities because it take too much energy to rebut. Again, we are putting ourselves out there if we do rebut.

THOM: Now this might sound strange, but being out is in some ways a reflection of our individual inner work—part of our inward journey, if you will. Like coming out, this inward journey is not a single event but rather a commitment for a lifetime. I mention this to suggest that you never feel guilty if you do not have the strength, energy, or inclination to rebut every slight or offensive comment directed to or about LGBTQ persons. None of us has that much emotional wherewithal. That is why I cannot take a hard stance for or against coming out in any context, including adult education classrooms. I can know only what is right for me, but I cannot presume that fits anyone else. Progressive and radical change occurs because of countless acts of everyday people who find ways to challenge those who hold power over them, and even in the smallest acts of protest can be found the invisible roots of social change (Zinn, 1994).

A Tentative Conclusion

Clearly we believe that the adult education classroom is an important context for dialogue about issues related to sexual orientation. We also believe that there is no clear answer for how individual faculty or students, no matter what their sexual orientation, should handle challenging the heteronormative. Everyone needs to make those decisions for herself or himself in the light of a host of factors mentioned above. But we keep in mind the following comment by Howard Zinn (1994, p. 33), which helps us to maintain perspective when few people attend conference presentations on LGBTQ issues or classroom discussions are not as engaging as perhaps we would like: "No pitifully small picket line, no poorly attended meeting, no tossing out of an idea to an audience or even to an individual should be scorned as insignificant." Change happens slowly and over time. It can happen by what

New Directions for Adult and Continuing Education • DOI: 10.1002/ace

occurs in one small classroom in rural Pennsylvania, urban Chicago, or suburban San Francisco. We are glad to be part of the dialogue.

References

Abalos, D. *La Communidad Latina in the United States.* Westport, Conn.: Praeger, 1998.

Griffin, P. *Strong Women, Deep Closets: Lesbian and Homophobia in Sport.* Champaign, Ill.: Human Kinetics, 1998.

Hill, R. J. "Activism as Practice: Some Queer Considerations." In R. St. Clair and J. A. Sandlin (eds.), *Promoting Critical Practice in Adult Education.* New Directions for Adult and Continuing Education, no. 102. San Francisco: Jossey-Bass, 2004.

hooks, b. *Teaching to Transgress: Education as the Practice of Freedom.* New York: Routledge, 1994.

Kissen, R. M. *The Last Closet: The Real Lives of Lesbian and Gay Teachers.* Portsmouth, N.H.: Heinemann, 1996.

Rich, A. "Compulsory Heterosexuality and Lesbian Existence." *Signs: Journal of Women in Culture and Society,* 1980, 5, 631–660.

Sedgwick, E. *Epistemology of the Closet.* Berkeley: University of California Press, 1990.

Tierney, W. G. *Academic Outlaws: Queer Theory and Cultural Studies in the Academy.* Thousand Oaks, Calif.: Sage, 1997.

Tisdell, E. J. "Feminist Perspectives on Adult Education: Constantly Shifting Identities in Constantly Shifting Times." In V. Sheared and P. A. Sissel (eds.), *Making Space: Merging Theory and Practice in Adult Education.* Westport, Conn.: Bergin & Garvey, 2001.

Yescavage, K., and Alexander, J. "The Pedagogy of Marking: Addressing Sexual Orientation in the Classroom." *Feminist Teacher,* 1997, 11(2), 113–122.

Zinn, H. *You Can't Be Neutral on a Moving Train: A Personal History of Our Times.* Boston: Beacon Press, 1994.

THOMAS V. BETTINGER *is a doctoral student in adult education at Penn State University–Harrisburg.*

REBECCA TIMMINS *is a doctoral student in adult education at Penn State University–Harrisburg.*

ELIZABETH J. TISDELL *is an associate professor of adult education at Penn State University–Harrisburg.*

New Directions for Adult and Continuing Education • DOI: 10.1002/ace

7

This chapter addresses recent changes in public policy and organizational practices that affect LGBTQ individuals and the role that organizational policy can play in establishing and maintaining respectful and inclusive workplaces.

Using Policy to Drive Organizational Change

Eunice Ellen Hornsby

Since the 1969 Stonewall riots gave birth to the gay rights movement, radical changes have occurred regarding awareness and acceptance of lesbian, gay, bisexual, transgender, and queer (LGBTQ) people. Gay pride marches, civil unions and gay marriage, adoption by LGBTQ individuals, statutes barring sexual orientation discrimination, health benefits for domestic partners, and popular televisions shows featuring prominent gay characters are just some evidence of these changes. These changes provoked fear and backlash in some quarters, spurring the November 2004 passage of eleven U.S. state ballot initiatives banning same-sex marriage. In the midst of such a culture war, it is crucial that organizations secure policy changes that protect LGBTQ individuals from discrimination and foster inclusion.

Other trends pressing for LGBTQ-inclusive workplace policies and practices include labor force constriction caused by baby boomer retirements, an emphasis on work/life balance and family-friendly employers, and expectations for acceptance of LGBTQ individuals by younger workers entering the labor market. Given the impending retirement of millions of baby boomers, employers in health and educational services, among others, face difficulties recruiting and retaining qualified workers (Dohm, 2000). Although 79 percent of baby boomers (American Association of Retired Persons, 2004) plan to work part time after retirement, employers will compete for this labor pool and will need to provide inclusive and flexible workplaces. Another trend in public and private sector employment is programs to promote greater work/life balance. Most of these focus predominantly on

NEW DIRECTIONS FOR ADULT AND CONTINUING EDUCATION, no. 112, Winter 2006 © 2006 Wiley Periodicals, Inc.
Published online in Wiley InterScience (www.interscience.wiley.com) • DOI: 10.1002/ace.238

child and elder care issues for heterosexuals. As more employers add domestic partner benefits and include sexual orientation in their nondiscrimination policies, it is essential to expand the definition of families served by work/life programs to include those of LGBTQ individuals. A small and growing number of employers are developing resources and policies to support and include transgender employees in the workplace (Human Rights Campaign Foundation, 2004).

Evolving Law and Public Policy

Black's Law Dictionary defines public policy broadly as "principles and standards regarded by the legislature or by the courts as being of fundamental concern to the state and the whole of society" (Garner, 1999, p. 1267). Public policy advances over the past 150 years have driven significant change in U.S. workplaces. Before 1863, public policy allowed citizens to own the people who staffed their businesses, a practice known as slavery. One hundred years later, Title VII of the Civil Rights Act of 1964 began twenty-six years of sweeping changes in federal public policy regarding employment discrimination. Title VII outlaws employment discrimination against individuals based on race, color, religion, sex, or national origin; the Equal Pay Act of 1963 protects women and men who perform substantially equal work in the same establishment from sex-based wage discrimination; the Age Discrimination in Employment Act of 1967 bars discrimination against individuals who are over age forty; and Title I of the Americans with Disabilities Act (1990) prohibits employment discrimination against individuals with disabilities. The 1998 presidential Executive Order 13087 prohibits discrimination based on sexual orientation within executive branch civilian employment; in 2000, Executive Order 13153 added "status as a parent" to the list of categories protected from discrimination in this same workforce. On September 14, 2005, the U.S. House of Representatives passed a federal hate crime bill that included lesbian, gay, bisexual, and transgender individuals, but it has not been passed by the Senate. The District of Columbia and fifteen states have laws prohibiting sexual orientation discrimination in private employment (California, Connecticut, Hawaii, Illinois, Maryland, Massachusetts, Minnesota, Nevada, New Hampshire, New Jersey, New Mexico, New York, Rhode Island, Vermont, and Wisconsin).

Public policy progress is occurring in Canada (see Chapter Five, this volume) and Europe as well. The Canadian Human Rights Act, applicable to federal employers, was amended in 1996 to include a prohibition of discrimination based on sexual orientation, added to its other categories including race, national or ethnic origin, color, religion, age, sex, marital status, family status, disability, or conviction for an offense for which a pardon has been granted (Canadian Human Rights Commission, 1996). In 2000, the Council of the European Communities adopted Directive 2000/78/EC requiring member states to take measures to prohibit employ-

New Directions for Adult and Continuing Education • DOI: 10.1002/ace

ment discrimination based on religion or belief, disability, age, or sexual orientation (European Commission, 2000). In May 2005, a bill was introduced into the Canadian House of Commons to include gender identity or expression as a category protected by the Canadian Human Rights Act (House of Commons of Canada, 2005).

Privacy and Equal Protection. Recent U.S. Supreme Court cases have expanded support for equal protection and the right to privacy on the basis of sexual orientation. In *Romer* v. *Evans* (1996), the U.S. Supreme Court held unconstitutional an amendment to the Colorado constitution, passed in a state referendum, denying protection from sexual orientation discrimination and forbidding reinstatement of state or local government laws that protect against sexual orientation discrimination. The Court held the amendment to be a violation of the equal protection clause because it lacked a rational relationship to legitimate state interests and it could not be explained by anything but animus toward homosexuals. In *Lawrence* v. *Texas* (2003, p. 567), the Supreme Court overturned its 1986 *Bowers* v. *Hardwick* decision upholding a Georgia sodomy law: "When sexuality finds overt expression in intimate conduct with another person, the conduct can be but one element in a personal bond that is more enduring. The liberty protected by the Constitution allows homosexual persons the right to make this choice." These cases mark an overall trend toward greater protection of the rights of LGBTQ persons as a function of the rights of privacy and equal protection.

Workplace Discrimination. In 1989, the Supreme Court expanded discrimination based on sex to include discrimination based on sex stereotypes: "As for the legal relevance of sex stereotyping we are beyond the day when an employer could evaluate employees by assuming or insisting that they matched the stereotype associated with their group." (*Price Waterhouse* v. *Hopkins*, p. 251). Fifteen years later, the Sixth Circuit Court of Appeals held that it was a mistake to conclude that transsexuals as a class are not afforded Title VII protection: "Sex stereotyping based on a person's gender non-conforming behavior is impermissible discrimination, irrespective of the cause of that behavior; a label, such as 'transsexual,' is not fatal to a sex discrimination claim where the victim has suffered discrimination because of his or her gender non-conformity" (*Smith* v. *City of Salem, Ohio*, 2004, p. 575). These cases demonstrate a small but growing acknowledgment that discrimination based on gender identity or expression is a form of sex discrimination and that remedies can be pursued through the courts.

Workplace Bullying. Motivated by widely promulgated Equal Employment Opportunity Commission guidance and fear of liability, many U.S. employers have vigorously pursued eliminating sexual harassment through preventive steps such as policy development and training and remedial steps such as corrective action or removal of harassers from the workplace. As employers have pursued the eradication of sexual harassment, they have learned of harassment based on sexual orientation and gender identity

New Directions for Adult and Continuing Education • DOI: 10.1002/ace

or expression, as well as bullying based on miscellaneous or no particular personal characteristic.

Workplace bullying, called mobbing or moral harassment in Europe, has been a growing field of study since the mid-1990s. It refers to harassment or hostility that occurs over time and has negative consequences for the individual at whom it is targeted (Keashly and Harvey, 2004). Research indicates that bullies generally occupy positions superior to their targets, with 71 percent of bullies in the United States and 75 percent of bullies in Europe outranking their targets (Namie, 2003; Hoel and Cooper, 2000).

Legislative activity on workplace bullying spans Europe and North America. Sweden enacted its Victimization at Work Ordinance in 1993; France addressed moral harassment in the workplace in its 2002 Social Modernization Law. Quebec Provincial Law—Labour Standards—enacted in 2004 addresses psychological harassment at work. In the United States, the Workplace Bullying and Trauma Institute has sponsored model legislation in several states, although none has been enacted into law. These legislative trends point to a growing awareness that harassment and abuse at work are bad for individuals and for business. This trend is a positive development for the LGBTQ community. As awareness of workplace bullying grows and the practice becomes less tolerated, those who are abused based on sexual orientation or gender identity or expression will benefit. Employers that take steps to eliminate harassment and bullying will reap the benefits of a workforce that is not distracted, damaged, or displaced by hostile or abusive treatment (Schneider, Swan, and Fitzgerald, 1997). (Chapter Eight, this volume, explores this issue.)

Trends in Organizational Policies and Practices

Public and private sector employers are implementing more inclusive policies and practices each year. According to the Human Rights Campaign Foundation (2005b), 82 percent of Fortune 500 firms include sexual orientation in their nondiscrimination policies, and 46 percent offer domestic partner benefits. In response to the foundation's Corporate Equality Index survey, 113 of 236 responding corporations include transgender discrimination protection, for an increase of 92 percent for 2005 over 2004 (Human Rights Campaign Foundation, 2005a).

As of March 2005, 2,867 public and private employers include sexual orientation in their equal employment opportunity or nondiscrimination policies, including 551 colleges and universities (Human Rights Campaign Foundation, 2005b). There are 8,276 public and private sector employers, including 130 city and county governments and 290 colleges and universities, that offer health insurance benefits for domestic partners of their employees, compared to 21 in 1989. Eleven states (Vermont, New York, Oregon, California, Connecticut, Rhode Island, Washington, Iowa, New Mexico, Illinois, and New Jersey) and the District of Columbia offer health

New Directions for Adult and Continuing Education • DOI: 10.1002/ace

insurance benefits for their employees' domestic partners (Human Rights Campaign Foundation, 2005b). As of December 2004, 201 private sector and college and university employers included gender identity or expression in their nondiscrimination policies (Human Rights Campaign Foundation, 2005b).

Organizational Policies

Public and private employers create workplaces that intentionally or unintentionally welcome or discourage the participation of LGBTQ individuals as employees, customers, and key stakeholders. Organizations inspire and focus their employees through their mission, vision, and values statements. A mission is a short, concise statement of the organization's business—for example, "We provide literacy education for individuals who speak English as their second language." If employees can easily state their organization's mission, it is a clear indicator that they know what they and others should focus on at work. A vision is a short, concise statement of where the organization hopes to grow; it is a powerful and positive future aspiration—for example, "Our company will be synonymous with wilderness education vacations in the Pacific Northwest." Missions address what organizations do, visions identify where they are going, and values identify what they believe about the nature of their work—for example, "We value entrepreneurism, creativity, risk-taking, and integrity in all our work."

Organizational policies put into practice the organization's mission, vision, and values and are a clearer expression of these key concepts than are the statements themselves. Policies and the organizational practices that grow out of them are where mission, vision, and values meet the test of action. Organizations hoping to recruit and retain high performers must ensure that all employees are welcomed and supported by their policies and practices. A policy is a planned course of action, a guiding principle, or a statement that directs action for an organization. Policies direct many aspects of organizational life; financial, human resources, information technology, and governance are a few examples. From organization to organization, policies vary in their orientation; however, most organizations develop policies that either attempt to control and sanction negative behavior (unexcused absences, inappropriate use of company resources, illegal discrimination) or encourage and reward positive behavior (regular attendance, community service, wellness activities, whistle-blowing).

Inclusive Policies. Although many organizations claim to value diversity, their policies encourage practices that deny access or benefits to LGBTQ or other individuals who may be different from those who develop or approve such policies. Intentional or not, these exclusionary practices have significant negative implications for many employees and can have a negative effect on performance. Studies across work settings have demonstrated that pleasant affect is a strong predictor of job performance: that happy

New Directions for Adult and Continuing Education • DOI: 10.1002/ace

employees are productive employees (Côte, 1999) and that job satisfaction is predictive of performance (Saari and Judge, 2004). (See also Chapter Eight, this volume.)

Exclusionary policies and practices often develop because of the lens through which the developers look. Most people see the world from one vantage point: their own. Policy developers must consider and incorporate many viewpoints in the policy development and implementation process if inclusivity of diversity is truly an organizational value and goal. But how does an organization accomplish this? First, it is crucial to document and publish the policy development process. Leaders, managers, employees, customers, and stakeholders should know the purpose that policies serve in the organization and the process used to draft, solicit feedback, and finalize any policy. Second, organizations must make explicit that policies support achieving the organization's vision and values and serve to include rather than exclude. Third, all efforts should be made to include those affected by the policies at the table as policies are being conceptualized or updated. Policies should be shared widely with managers, employees, and constituency groups for feedback prior to finalization. There is risk in this practice; individuals and groups may be disappointed when all of their feedback is not integrated. However, it is far riskier to develop and implement policies without input from the managers and employees that they are designed to serve. Finally, organizations should develop tools and processes to ensure that all individuals involved in policy development, implementation, and interpretation are sensitized to varying effects on LGBTQ and other individuals who are different from the cultural or organizational norm.

LGBTQ Policy Inclusivity Checklist. One approach to sensitize individuals to discriminatory effects of a policy is to develop a checklist to be used by all involved in the policy development process. This checklist should apply to policies and accompanying procedures, forms, implementation guides, and frequently-asked-question documents, as well as any other advice or guidance disseminated by the organization on policy issues. As policies are developed, consider these guidelines:

- Use *partner* or *significant other* in place of *spouse.*
- Use *employee, staff,* or other gender-neutral terms instead of gendered pronouns such as *she, he, her,* and *him.*
- Use inclusive-gender pronouns rather than *I* and *male,* such as *one, you, they,* and *their.*
- If *family, immediate family, household,* or other such terms are used, define them to include domestic partners, children of the partnership, and relatives of the partnership that parallel relatives of married couples (parents-in-law, brother- or sister-in-law, daughter- or son-in-law, and so forth). Place the definition at the beginning of any document using these terms.
- Are benefits and privileges conferred based on marital status? If so, extend them to nontraditional families. Limit any differences in benefits and

privileges based on marital status to those explicitly mandated by statute or administrative regulation, such as federal or state tax regulations. Include an explanation of why such differences exist.

• If proof of family relationship is required, are equitable levels of proof required of married and nonmarried families? For example, if domestic partners are required to submit an affidavit of domestic partnership, are married couples required to submit a marriage certificate? Are the requirements for the affidavit similar to the requirements for a marriage license? If not, equalize the requirements.

• Are sexual orientation and gender identity or expression included in equal opportunity, harassment and bullying, and nondiscrimination policies? If not, include them.

• What training or education do managers and employees need to enable them to adhere to the spirit as well as the letter of the policy? How will the organization ensure that reticent managers and employees participate?

• Do dress guidelines emphasize professional attire while avoiding rigid sex role stereotypes and expectations?

• Do health insurance policies exclude gender reassignment and confirmation procedures? If so, explore including such procedures.

• Are processes in place to ensure that transitioning employees can change their name and sex in organizational records and that they will have convenient and safe locker and toilet facilities?

All policies, programs, and benefits should be reviewed for LGBTQ bias. Although bias will show up in many policies and practices, those that are especially vulnerable to heterosexual bias should be given special scrutiny. The largest class consists of those that confer access to benefits or privileges based on family relationship, including health benefits, child care, retirement benefits and programs, relocation and support for dual-career couples, employee assistance programs, company fitness facility membership, work/life services, and inclusion in company activities for family members. In these cases, access should be cost and requirement neutral for LGBTQ individuals. Other policies that commonly discriminate based on sexual orientation or gender identity or expression and should be reviewed for such discriminatory impact include dress codes and guidelines, family medical leave, parental or adoption leave, sick leave, bereavement leave, sexual harassment, consensual relationships and dating, nepotism, and domestic or relationship and workplace violence.

The purpose of policy is to state organizational beliefs and expectations for management and employee practice, encourage desired performance, and minimize undesirable behavior. Accountability is necessarily a part of this. For policies that may not be popularly accepted by managers and employees, accountability strategies and measures are crucial. Organizations must guard against developing and disseminating policies for the sake of public relations and must be prepared to hold accountable those managers and employees who choose to operate outside articulated guidelines and expectations.

Implementing Policies: Domestic Partner Benefits. Many organizations that offer domestic partner health benefits require an affidavit of domestic partnership, and these same organizations do not always require that married individuals submit a marriage certificate. One might assume that organizations that offer health insurance benefits for domestic partners would be concerned about discrimination manifest through the processes established to qualify for such benefits; however, this is not the case. Common statutory requirements for marriage include age, ability to consent, not currently married, not related closer than first cousins (with some exceptions), and up to a five-day waiting period. Common requirements of affidavits of domestic partnership imposed by employers include (1) declaration of a permanent relationship; (2) joint financial or estate planning documents; (3) joint ownership of major assets; (4) joint liabilities or debts; (5) partner designated as beneficiary of will, retirement plan, or insurance policy; (6) durable powers of attorney designating powers to the partner; (7) three- to six-month waiting period; and (8) joint permanent residence (Hornsby, 2005). Such requirements cause LGBTQ employees to shoulder extra financial burdens as they prepare and submit legal documents, encourage assumption of debt and major purchases when they may be inappropriate, and otherwise require differential treatment of LGBTQ employees as compared to their heterosexual married counterparts. How would married individuals respond if, to qualify for health insurance coverage for their spouse, they were required by their employer to own property or assume debt in particular ways, engage in financial or estate planning, give their spouse general power of attorney, and wait for six months after they are married for such insurance coverage? These significantly different requirements of married versus same-sex partners are a common example of how policies that intend positive outcomes in fact discriminate against the very population they were developed to include or advance. In addition, they are classic examples of heterosexism: the privileging of heterosexuality.

Implementing Policies: Transitioning in the Workplace. Although issues may arise at any time, the point at which a transsexual begins her or his trial living period in the reassigned gender, referred to as transitioning, presents numerous issues if an employee remains in the workplace (Rose, 2004; Walworth, 2003). How we respond to individuals is inextricably tied to their presenting gender; everything we do from the moment we are born is in some way influenced by our gender and how others respond to it (Rocco and Gallagher, 2005). When an individual transitions, coworkers will experience varying degrees of discomfort and confusion. Organizations are better served preparing for these issues in advance than to be caught unprepared when a male employee walks through the door and says, "I need to change my company ID. Next week

New Directions for Adult and Continuing Education • DOI: 10.1002/ace

I will be coming to work as a woman."

How does an employer prepare? Integrating gender identity or expression in harassment, discrimination, and equal employment opportunity policies is a first step. As these policies are updated, the organization should provide managers and employees with education and tools such as definitions of terms, frequently asked questions, guidelines for transitioning employees, employee assistance program interventions, consultation, and community or Web-based resources. Including the issue in climate, diversity, and antidiscrimination training or initiatives is crucial. Many individuals have had no exposure to transgender issues or education and are naturally uncomfortable with the unfamiliar, different, or that which is "queer."

Best practice indicates that transitioning employees use the restroom consistent with their presenting gender. For many coworkers, this will be uncomfortable. Include gender-neutral or single-unit restroom facilities when building or renovating facilities. These restrooms easily fulfill ADA requirements. Individuals with disabilities and individuals with children will be grateful, and organizations that use them will be a step ahead of the restroom issue that inevitably comes up when employees transition.

It is crucial to have open and frank discussions about issues that may come up when an employee transitions. Supervisors and human resource professionals should clearly and sensitively articulate the organization's expectations about what behaviors are acceptable in the workplace and should offer strategies for constructively addressing emotional issues. The transition will be a challenging time. Organizations that facilitate it through open and respectful discussion, expectation setting, and appropriate support for the individual and coworkers will reinforce an environment that engenders respect for all. It is most effective to emphasize creating an environment in which individual employees are able to contribute their best work rather than "accepting Davida *even though* he/she is different." This focus on respect and inclusion for business purposes will serve the organization well the next time an individual who is different is introduced into the workplace, whether the difference is based on gender, disability, religion, or some other variable.

Conclusion

Changing an organization's nondiscrimination policy to include sexual orientation and gender identity or expression is the first step, and for some organizations it is a challenging one. Changing a few words in a policy is an important public statement of support for and inclusion of GLTBQ individuals. If an organization desires culture change, leaders, managers, and employees must be educated, provided with tools to support constructive workplace performance, and held accountable if they remain outside the realm of organizational expectations.

New Directions for Adult and Continuing Education • DOI: 10.1002/ace

Organizations can use policies and the accompanying training to operationalize their mission, vision, and values. Creating inclusive and forward-thinking policies and preparing leaders, managers, and employees to live the spirit as well as the letter of policies will yield volumes through the creation of workplaces that challenge all individuals to do their best work because of, rather than in spite of, who they truly are.

References

American Association of Retired Persons. "Baby Boomers Envision Retirement II—Key Findings." 2004. http://www.aarp.org/research/reference/boomers/aresearch-import-865.html. Accessed Mar. 20, 2006.

Bowers v. Hardwick. (1986). 478 U.S. 186.

Canadian Human Rights Commission. Annual Report. 1996. http://www.chrc-ccdp.ca/publications/1996_ar/page8-en.asp. Accessed July 7, 2006.

Côte, S. "Affect and Performance in Organizational Settings." Current Directions in Psychological Science, 1999, 8(2), 65–68.

Dohm, A. "Gauging the Labor Force Effects of Retiring Baby-Boomers." Monthly Labor Review, 2000, 123(7), 17–25. http://www.bls.gov/opub/mlr/2000/07/art2full.pdf. Accessed Mar. 20, 2006.

European Commission. "Council Directive 2000/78/EC of 27 November 2000." http://ec.europa.eu/employment_social/news/2001/jul/dir200078_en.html. Accessed Jul. 7, 2006.

Garner, B. A. Blacks Law Dictionary. (8th ed.) St. Paul, Minn.: West Publishing, 1999.

Hoel, H., and Cooper, C. "Destructive Conflict and Bullying at Work." 2000. http://www.csren.gov.uk/UMISTreportHelgeHoel1.PDF. Accessed Mar. 20, 2006.

Hornsby, E. E. "Marriage, Domestic Partnership, and Employment Benefits: What Does Equality Mean in Public Higher Education?" Working paper, Ohio State University, 2005.

House of Commons of Canada. "Bill C-392: An Act to Amend the Canadian Human Rights Act (Gender Identity)." 2005. http://www.parl.gc.ca/38/1/parlbus/chambus/house/bills/private/C-392/C-392_1/C-392_cover-F.html. Accessed July 7, 2006.

Human Rights Campaign Foundation. Transgender Issues in the Workplace: A Tool for Managers. 2004. http://www.hrc.org/. Accessed Mar. 20, 2006.

Human Rights Campaign Foundation. Corporate Equality Index: A Report Card on Gay, Lesbian, Bisexual and Transgender Equality in Corporate America. 2005a. http://www.hrc.org/. Accessed Mar. 20, 2006.

Human Rights Campaign Foundation. The State of the Workplace for Lesbian, Gay, Bisexual, and Transgender Americans-2004. 2005b. http://www.hrc.org/. Accessed Mar. 20, 2006.

Keashly, L., and Harvey, S. "Emotional Abuse in the Workplace." In P. Spector and S. Fox (eds.), Counterproductive Work Behavior: Investigations of Actors and Targets. Washington, D.C.: American Psychological Association, 2004.

Lawrence v. Texas. (2003). 539 U.S. 558, 567

Namie, G. The WBTI 2003 Report on Abusive Workplaces. 2003. http://www.bullyinginstitute.org/res/2003toc.html. Accessed Mar. 20, 2006.

Price Waterhouse v. Hopkins. (1989). 490 U.S. 228, 251.

Rocco, T. S., and Gallagher, S. (2005). "Straight Privilege, Moral/izing, and Myths: The Effects on Learners, Educational Options, and Teaching for Social Justice." Unpublished manuscript.

Romer v. Evans. (1996). 517 U.S. 620, 865–866.

Rose, D. *Transsexuals in the Workplace: A Survivor's Perspective.* 2004. http://www.don-narose.com/TranssexualsInTheWorkplace.pdf. Accessed Mar. 24, 2006.

Saari, L. M., and Judge, T. A. "Employee Attitudes and Job Satisfaction." *Human Resource Management,* 2004, *43*(4), 395–407. www.interscience.wiley.com. Accessed Mar. 20, 2006.

Schneider, K. T., Swan, S., and Fitzgerald, L. F. "Job-Related and Psychological Effects of Sexual Harassment in the Workplace: Empirical Evidence from Two Organizations." *Journal of Applied Psychology,* 1997, *82*(3), 401–415.

Smith v. *City of Salem, Ohio.* (2004). 378 F.3d 566, 575 (6th Cir.).

Walworth, J. *Managing Transsexual Transition in the Workplace.* 2003. http://www.gendersanity.com/shrm.html. Accessed Mar. 20, 2006.

EUNICE ELLEN HORNSBY is an organization development consultant and coordinates human resource policies with the Ohio State University, Columbus.

8

This chapter outlines the unique experiences of gay and lesbians in organizational settings and offers best practices for human resource professionals in supporting their sexual minority employees.

LGBTQ Issues in Organizational Settings: What HRD Professionals Need to Know and Do

Corey S. Muñoz, Kecia M. Thomas

Although heterosexual people dominate the workforce, the number of sexual minorities is significant, placed at between 10 and 14 percent (Powers, 1996). To help put these numbers in perspective, other minority groups such as racial and ethnic minorities often make up lower proportions of the American workforce, for example, Asian Americans (4 percent) and Hispanic Americans (10 percent). Therefore, a significant proportion of the workforce may have a nonheterosexual identity and potentially suffer from discrimination, harassment, exclusion, and isolation because of it. Lesbian, gay, bisexual, transgender, and queer (LGBTQ) workers may suffer psychologically and professionally due to hostile workplaces. Furthermore, when consideration is given that a sexual minority could also be a member of a racial minority, a woman, disabled, or economically or educationally disenfranchised, the importance of understanding this marginalized population is magnified.

This chapter outlines ways in which the LGBTQ population may confront hostile workplaces due to overt and covert instances of discrimination. Increasingly however, according to the Human Rights Campaign (HRC), organizations are taking steps to make their workplaces safe environments for all workers. Therefore, we will examine the best practices from organizations and firms that have excelled at creating safe workplaces and conclude by describing the importance of creating hospitable work environments.

New Directions for Adult and Continuing Education, no. 112, Winter 2006 © 2006 Wiley Periodicals, Inc.
Published online in Wiley InterScience (www.interscience.wiley.com) • DOI: 10.1002/ace.239

Discrimination and Heterosexist Privilege in the Workplace

Given that discrimination against LGBTQ workers is not explicitly illegal under any federal legislation (although protection could potentially be afforded in a number of cases by some existing federal laws; see Chapter Seven, this issue), the Equal Employment Opportunity Commission (EEOC) does not track discrimination or harassment as a result of one's sexual identity status. Yet individual organizations are knowledgeable about the extent to which LGBTQ workers experience intimidation and violence. Organizations, however, are less aware of the extent to which heterosexism, and the privileges that come with it, creates unequal opportunities for heterosexual and homosexual workers.

Overt discriminatory behaviors may be more common toward sexual minorities given that they are not protected under federal civil rights law, as are racial minorities and women. However, egalitarian and emerging norms for equal rights for sexual minorities have begun to limit overt forms of discrimination. Heterosexism has been defined as an ideological system that denies, denigrates, and stigmatizes all nonheterosexual forms of behavior, relationships, or communities (Herek, 1990). Just as in other theories and forms of prejudice, heterosexism can manifest itself in formal or interpersonal ways (Fernald, 1995; Hebl, Foster, Mannix, and Dovidio, 2002). Formal discrimination includes institutional and societal customs that discriminate against individual sexual minorities. Formal discrimination could also include discrimination in the hiring process, promotion, access, and resource distribution (Hebl, Foster, Mannix, and Dovidio, 2002; Chung, 2001). In contrast, interpersonal discrimination is subtle and includes verbal and nonverbal behaviors that occur in social interactions (Fernald, 1995; Hebl, Foster, Mannix, and Dovidio, 2002). Manifestations of interpersonal discrimination may include limiting behaviors toward sexual minorities such as showing less interest, limited interaction, and demonstrating negative attitudes toward homosexuals.

Another perspective that sheds light on the experiences of gay and lesbian employees is heterosexist privilege. *Privilege* has many definitions but can be best described as those everyday activities, rules, laws, and situations that create opportunities or advantages for those who fit the characteristics of the defined norm or status quo and disadvantages for those who lack those characteristics and do not conform to society's expectations. These characteristics include race, gender, sexuality, and physical ability or disability (Wildman and Davis, 1995). Peggy McIntosh (1993) views privilege as an invisible package of unearned assets that the privileged can count on cashing in each day.

Perhaps privilege is best explained by behavioral examples. For instance, an illustration of white privilege could be turning on the television or opening the front page of the newspaper and seeing only people of your own (dominant) race widely and positively represented (McIntosh,

New Directions for Adult and Continuing Education • DOI: 10.1002/ace

1993). Heterosexist privilege might include heterosexuals being able to express affection (for example, by hugging or holding hands) in social situations without hostile or violent reactions from others. A common example of workplace privilege is for heterosexuals being able to place pictures of loved ones on their desks or the freedom to acknowledge their relationship or family without having to think of the potential negative consequences of such an action.

Another type of discrimination that sexual minorities often confront involves distancing. LGBTQ workers confront interpersonal discrimination when they are distanced from heterosexual supervisors, peers, and, at times, subordinates. Distancing behaviors are often used as an index of negative responses to minority groups (Lott and Maluso, 1995; Muñoz, 2003). There are a variety of ways in which heterosexuals create distance between themselves and the LGBTQ community, physically as well as psychologically. For example, one study found that heterosexuals perceive homosexuals as dissimilar to themselves (Shaffer and Wallace, 1990) and often limit future interactions with someone labeled as gay or lesbian (Krulewitz and Nash, 1980). Additional research found heterosexuals less willing to disclose and seek out information from a sexual minority coworker (Kite and Deaux, 1986).

Social distancing by heterosexual workers toward LGBTQ employees in the workplace has the potential to limit gay workers' upward mobility and professional development (see Chapter Five, this volume). When heterosexuals distance themselves from gay employees psychologically or physically, it denies LGBTQ workers opportunities that stem from heterosexual privilege. LGBTQ employees who are distanced in the workplace lack access to heterosexual networks that provide important performance and socialization information. Likewise, lack of mentoring, because of interpersonal discrimination, creates a void for LGBTQ workers who desire and need advocates, career counselors, and role models in their organizations. The lack of developmental opportunities that are afforded by relationships with heterosexual supervisors and peers subsequently limit LGBTQ workers' chances to excel, be noticed, and be promoted. Furthermore, if organizations allow interpersonal discrimination to persist by their silence or through reinforcement of LGTBQ distancing, the organization eventually loses this talent due to LGBTQ employee disengagement and subsequent attrition.

Best Practices for Supporting LGBTQ Workers

As our knowledge about the unique and complex workplace experiences of LGBTQ workers expands, so does the need for guidance and best practices for supporting these workers. Research by the HRC suggests that activity related to the LGBTQ workforce has increased significantly. Here we outline the best of these activities in supporting and creating an inclusive environment for all workers. Many of the recommendations offered have previously been suggested as strategies for supporting women and people of color. Yet there are also unique strategies to support diversity work that will benefit LGBTQ workers. Specifically, best practices for supporting LGBTQ workers are setting the context, preparing for resistance, leadership commitment, affinity and resource groups, and creating opportunities for continuous learning.

Setting the Context. Human resource practices provide the background for how employees, gay and straight, learn the organization's values regarding inclusion and diversity. Therefore, antidiscrimination and harassment policies that include sexual orientation and the provision of domestic partner benefits teach all organizational members about the extent to which LGBTQ workers are respected and valued. In order to avoid secondary victimization (Murphy, 2001), it is important that organizations clearly articulate employees' avenues for filing grievances or reporting instances of harassment or discrimination.

The response of a twenty-one-year veteran employee of a large technology software company provides a good example of standing behind an organization's diversity policies, even when sexual identity issues are included (see Hatch, Hall, and Kobata, 2004). After this company began to display diversity posters (some of which included gay workers), the employee posted two biblical scriptures condemning homosexuality in his work cubicle that were visible to both peers and customers. After repeated requests to remove the postings, he was fired for insubordination. He sued his company for religious discrimination in violation of Title VII and local state law. The U.S. Court of Appeals for the Ninth Circuit rejected his claim that his company was attempting to convert Christians to its values. Rather, the court stated, "all that the managers did was explain [the company's] diversity program to [the employee] and ask him to treat his coworkers with respect. . . . and not violate the company's harassment policy" (Hatch, Hall, and Kobata, 2004, p. 16).

Domestic partner benefits are one way to signal to employees and future employees that LGBTQ workers are valued in the organization. Mills (2000) reports that competitive benefits packages are key in attracting the best employees, and according to a 1999 survey by the Society for Human Resource Management and Commerce Clearing House, "domestic partner benefits were ranked as the number one most effective recruiting incentive for executives and the number three most effective recruiting incentive for managers and line workers" (p. 13). In addition to these benefits, organizations help to set the context for sexual identity diversity by including sexual orientation in diversity training, becoming involved in LGBTQ charitable organizations in their communities, and engaging in marketing efforts to the LGBTQ community (Mills, 2000).

Preparing for Resistance. A common mistake that diversity proponents confront, especially in regard to the inclusion of LGBTQ issues, is to underestimate the level of homophobia and heterosexism that exists throughout the organization (Fletcher and Kaplan, 2000). The mere mention of LGBTQ workers' presence as a workplace reality breaks the "cycle of invisibility that so insidiously inhibits progress on the issues" (Fletcher and Kaplan, 2000). Taking steps to break this invisibility and legitimize the LGBTQ population and its concerns and needs may unearth fears, bigotry, and hatred that had mostly been underground.

Early in one organization's efforts to make sexual orientation a workplace issue, a regional manager attempted to hold focus groups with gay workers. Despite the use of an external facilitator and several safeguards to protect participant identity, no one showed up. This was the company's first message that the climate for gay and lesbian workers might be hostile. The second message came when subsequent focus groups, conducted to assess the overall climate for all workers, revealed that gay workers were invisible and that it was acceptable to tell gay jokes in their workplace (Henneman, 2004). These efforts represent the underlying prejudice confronted by gay workers prior to the company's inclusive diversity campaign. Fletcher and Kaplan (2000, p. 33) provide further striking examples of the resistance that four corporate clients confronted after their campaign for supporting LGBTQ workers was launched:

Employees repeatedly defacing rainbow flag magnets and pink triangles (symbols of gay rights placed on office name plates to denote a safe space for discussing issues of sexual orientation)

Members of diversity councils and openly GLBT employees receiving hate email and voicemail—even implied death threats

An openly lesbian employee having her tires slashed in the parking lot of a hotel while she was participating in a diversity workshop

A group of religious fundamentalists circulating a petition protesting the extension of health benefits to the domestic partners of GLBT employees because they believed that the leaders "had gone too far"

Numerous examples of GLBT employees being mistreated or slighted, often openly and with no fear on the part of the perpetrators

While sensitizing top leaders on homophobia, heterosexism, and resistance, these consultants also started building skills in this management team in order to deal with the resistance before it began to emerge and derail diversity efforts. Resistance can be subtle or overt (Thomas, forthcoming). Subtle forms of resistance create anxiety and confusion for its targets as well as for the observer. Resistance can be so subtle that to object to it or confront it can lead targets to being labeled as overly sensitive or paranoid (Fletcher and Kaplan, 2000; Friedman and Davidson, 2001). Resistance to LGBTQ concerns or initiatives, however, is likely to be overt and visible given the lack of social sanctions against homophobia. Therefore, senior leaders have the opportunity to confront overt instances of LGBTQ resistance by restating their commitment for equity, having top leaders partner with LGBTQ interest groups to support their efforts, or engaging in systemwide training and workshops regarding inclusion and resistance (Fletcher and Kaplan, 2000).

Leadership Commitment. Without the understanding and commitment of top leadership, diversity efforts fail (Thomas, 2005; Jayne and Dipboye, 2004). This seems especially true of the inclusion of LGBTQ concerns in larger diversity strategies. For leaders who want to take on these issues, preparations must be made. Leaders also need to be able to effectively frame the organizational conversation around LGBTQ and larger diversity goals as being related to business goals (Jayne and Dipboye, 2004). For example, a director of diversity at a large financial institution addressed the business case for sexual orientation as a workplace issue: "It's a very tight labor market and if they [the company] want people to stay here, they have to move with the times. You have your ten benchmark companies and you have to implement these best practices if you're going to be competitive. People aren't going to work in a place where they don't think they'll be valued or included" (Obear, 2000, pp. 29–30).

Making the business case for diversity also means that leadership must include diversity in how those responsible for it are rewarded. A director of diversity at a health care company states, "It is critical to hold managers accountable for the work climate in their areas by changing performance appraisals and linking their bonus monies and merit raises to clear, measurable goals. . . . If you want to change an organization, grab the leaders by their wallets" (Obear, 2000, p. 27).

Leaders need to be present and participate in diversity initiatives, including training. One of the ways in which a large technology company has been successful in its diversity efforts, which includes the concerns of the LGBTQ community, is that the top leadership team has always been heavily involved in all diversity efforts (Thomas, 2005). This company has changed dramatically within the past ten years; for example, the number of self-identified gay, lesbian, bisexual, and transgender executives has increased by 733 percent (Thomas, 2005). The success of the technology company's diversity campaign has largely to do with the level of involvement that top leadership has in its diversity task force as well as in its affinity groups. In fact, a top manager is involved with every affinity group in order to learn the unique realities of being a group member in this organization, as well as to be able to push forward the agenda of each of these resource groups.

Affinity and Resource Groups. Conklin (2000) describes affinity groups (she uses the term *employee resource groups*) as a foundation for support and change regarding LGBTQ in organizations. The major vehicle by which affinity groups support the careers and presence of LGBTQ workers is through the provision of safe spaces to discuss their identity and its role in their work lives. Often these groups start informally; as membership grows, they seek the support and commitment of allies who are influential in the organization (Conklin, 2000). Conklin (2000, p. 15) suggests that affinity groups add value to the organization in a number of ways:

New Directions for Adult and Continuing Education • DOI: 10.1002/ace

To create a more equitable and safe work environment for GLBT employees

To increase awareness and education of all employees about sexual orientation as a workplace issue

To increase the retention of GLBT employees

To work with the organization to include sexual orientation in relevant personnel policies and practices, including offering domestic partner benefits

To increase employee recruitment within the gay community

To provide a network that supports the professional development of GLBT employees

These groups can become a powerful proponent of including sexual orientation in diversity training and all other diversity initiatives (Conklin, 2000). In some organizations, members of these resource groups provide advice and counsel to organizations regarding organizational policies that do not include sexual orientation (Obear, 2000). A manager at a large petroleum company indicated that affinity groups have had a significant impact on the organizational lives of LGBTQ employees: "It's [the GLBT network] been a hugely positive thing in many respects. It has provided a support structure for individuals who may have felt isolated or part of a small minority and given them an infrastructure for ongoing support. It has given those individuals a forum in which to raise concerns they have from their particular viewpoint that might not otherwise have received the level of exposure and attention they deserve. And it's given senior leaders exposure that they would not otherwise have" (quoted in Conklin, 2000, p. 16).

Continuous Learning. The inclusion of diversity training is significant to legitimize the concerns of the LGBT community in organizations, sensitize the organization to these issues, and provide all workers with the skills to collaborate successfully in a diverse and inclusive work environment. Team building and group process training are important skills for managers and diversity advocates to learn as they help organizations move forward in their diversity efforts (Jayne and Dipboye, 2004). Members of LGBTQ affinity groups often take the lead in providing training or making available speakers' bureaus to help promote learning about diversity in their organizations (Obear, 2000).

Learning about diversity and LGBTQ issues should do more than entail training. Organizations should work to monitor the climate for diversity within their organizations to understand trouble spots that may affect diverse workers (Jayne and Dipboye, 2004). Obear (2000) uses a large financial institution as a model of having continuous assessment regarding diversity issues in organizations: ". . . Diversity managers at [this company] continually gather information about the workplace climate through focus groups, individual conversations and incidents reported. They track the patterns and dynamics in business units, and provide feedback and consultation to managers about how to remedy situations" (p. 27).

New Directions for Adult and Continuing Education • DOI: 10.1002/ace

Organizational Benefits of Supporting LGBTQ Issues

In the HRC annual report on corporate policies on LGBT employees, the "State of the Workplace" (2004) document surveyed many Fortune 500 and privately held companies regarding laws and policies surrounding sexual orientation and gender identity and expression in the workplace. There appears to be a continuum in regard to affirming policies and practices for sexual minority employees, ranging from employee policies covering sexual orientation to employer-provided domestic partnership benefits. In addition, there is a gradual increase in affirming actions toward sexual orientation by organizations. For example, the report noted that an increase of 18 percent of companies they surveyed, as well as a total of 200 companies in the Fortune 500, an increase of 14 percent from the previous year, offer domestic partner benefits. The news is more positive with employer policies covering sexual orientation, with 360 companies in the Fortune 500, or 72 percent, including sexual orientation in their written nondiscrimination policy. In addition, 49 of the Fortune 50 include sexual orientation in their nondiscrimination policy, indicating that the closer the company is to the top of the Fortune list, the more likely it is to have inclusive policies.

Outcomes of Best Practices for Sexual Minority Workers

Because there is no specific federal protection against discrimination toward sexual minorities, statements of nondiscrimination are usually the only indication that discriminatory behaviors will not be tolerated within an organization. Researchers demonstrate the benefits of such statements showing that organizations that include sexual orientation in their nondiscrimination statements reduce discrimination toward their gay and lesbian employees and increase positive work attitudes of gays and lesbians (Button, 2001). Also, these organizational efforts to promote diversity have been linked to a more positive working environment for gay and lesbian employees. This positive social climate has been directly related to how open a gay or lesbian employee can be in the workplace in regard to sexuality. The organizational implication of this increased positive social environment is higher job satisfaction among sexual minorities (Ellis and Riggle, 1995). Not only is this level of "outness" related to job satisfaction, but a positive relationship has been shown between a positive organizational climate for sexual minorities and an increase in organizational commitment, lower job stress, and increased perception of top-level management support (Day and Schoenrade, 1997, 2000). Also, these organizational efforts have been shown to reduce workplace discrimination toward gays and lesbians (Ragins and Cornwell, 2001). The reduction of discrimination is related to job satisfaction, as most gay and lesbian employees still fear various forms of discrimination in the workplace (Levine and Leonard, 1984; Croteau, 1996).

Conclusion

The visibility of the LGBTQ population in our working environments is increasing rapidly. With this increase in visibility, these workers often confront overt and covert instances of discrimination in their working environments. However, many successful organizations have taken necessary steps and adopted inclusionary practices to help make their working environments safe for all their employees.

This chapter has focused on best practices for HRD professionals, including setting the context for learning inclusion and diversity within an organization, being proactive by preparing for resistance that often is associated with the diversity change process, gaining leadership commitment by holding managers accountable for their working climate, establishing affinity or employee resource groups to help establish a support structure for LGBTQ employees, and creating a continuous learning environment by the inclusion of diversity training. HRD professionals who adapt these best practices can benefit their organization by increasing the job satisfaction and organizational commitment of their LGBTQ employees, as well as helping to reduce discrimination in their organization.

References

Button, S. B. "Organizational Efforts to Affirm Sexual Diversity: A Cross-Level Examination." *Journal of Applied Psychology*, 2001, *86*(1), 17–28.

Chung, Y. B. "Work Discrimination and Coping Strategies: Conceptual Frameworks for Counseling Lesbian, Gay and Bisexual Clients." *Career Development Quarterly*, 2001, *50*, 33–44.

Conklin, W. "Employee Resource Groups: A Foundation for Support and Change." *Diversity Factor*, 2000, *9*(1), 15–24.

Croteau, J. M. "Research on the Work Experiences of Lesbian, Gay, and Bisexual People: An Integrative Review of Methodology and Findings." *Journal of Vocational Behavior*, 1996, *48*, 195–209.

Day, N. E., and Schoenrade, P. "Staying in the Closet Versus Coming Out: Relationships Between Communication About Sexual Orientation and Work Attitudes." *Personnel Psychology*, 1997, *50*, 147–163.

Day, N. E., and Schoenrade, P. "The Relationship Among Reported Disclosure of Sexual Orientation, Anti-Discrimination Policies, Top Management Support and Work Attitudes of Gay and Lesbian Employees." *Personnel Review*, 2000, *29*(3), 346–363.

Ellis, A. L., and Riggle, E.D.B. "The Relation of Job Satisfaction and Degree of Openness About One's Sexual Orientation for Lesbians and Gay Men." *Journal of Homosexuality*, 1995, *30*(2), 75–85.

Fernald, J. L. "Interpersonal Heterosexism." In B. Lott and D. Maluso (eds.), *The Social Psychology of Interpersonal Discrimination*. New York: Guilford Press, 1995.

Fletcher, S., and Kaplan, M. "The Diversity Change Process: Integrating Sexual Orientation." *Diversity Factor,* 2000, 9(1), 31–36.

Friedman, R., and Davidson, M. "Managing Diversity and Second-Order Conflict," *International Journal of Conflict Management,* 2001, 12(2), 132–153.

Hatch, D. D., Hall, J. E., and Kobata, M. T. "Anti-Gay Postings at Work Not Protected." *Workforce Management,* 2004, 83(3), 16.

Hebl, M. R., Foster, J. B., Mannix, L. M., and Dovidio, J. F. "Formal and Interpersonal Discrimination: A Field Study of Bias Toward Homosexual Applicants." *Personality and Social Psychology Bulletin,* 2002, 28(6), 815–825.

Henneman, T. "Acceptance of Gays, Lesbians Is a Big Part of Kodak's Diversity Picture." *Workforce Management,* 2004, 83(13), 68–70.

Herek, G. M. "The Context of Anti-Gay Violence: Notes on Cultural and Psychological Heterosexism." *Journal of Interpersonal Violence,* 1990, 5(3), 316–333.

Human Rights Campaign. *State of the Workplace for Lesbian, Gay, Bisexual, and Transgender Americans.* Washington, D.C.: Human Rights Campaign, 2004.

Jayne, M., and Dipboye, R. "Leveraging Diversity to Improve Business Performance: Research Findings and Recommendations for Organizations." *Human Resource Management,* Winter 2004, 43(4), 409–424.

Kite, M. E., and Deaux, K. "Attitudes Toward Homosexuality: Assessment and Behavioral Consequences." *Basic and Applied Social Psychology,* 1986, 7(2), 137–162.

Kite, M. E., and Whitley, B. E. *Stigma and Sexual Orientation: Understanding Prejudice Against Lesbians, Gay Men, and Bisexuals.* Thousand Oaks, Calif.: Sage, 1998.

Krulewitz, J. E., and Nash, J. E. "Effects of Sex-Role Attitudes and Similarity on Men's Rejection of Male Homosexuals." *Journal of Personality and Social Psychology,* 1980, 38(1), 67–74.

Levine, M. P., and Leonard, R. "Discrimination Against Lesbians in the Workforce." *Signs: Journal of Women in Culture and Society,* 1984, 9, 700–710.

Lott, B., and Maluso, D. (eds.). *The Social Psychology of Interpersonal Discrimination.* New York: Guilford Press, 1995.

McIntosh, P. "White Privilege and Male Privilege: A Personal Account of Coming to See Correspondences Through Work in Women's Studies." In A. Minas (ed.), *Gender Basics.* Belmont, Calif.: Wadsworth, 1993.

Mills, K. I. "GLBT Employees Make Gains in Workplaces Nationwide." *Diversity Factor,* 2000, 9(1), 11–14.

Muñoz, C. S. "Intergroup Anxiety and Willingness to Partner: Heterosexual Response to Sexual Minority Co-Workers." Unpublished master's thesis, University of Georgia, 2003.

Murphy, B. C. "Anti-Gay/Lesbian Violence in the United States." In D. J. Christie, R. V. Wagner, and D. D. Winter (eds.), *Peace, Conflict, and Violence: Peace Psychology for the Twenty-First Century.* Upper Saddle River, N.J.: Prentice Hall, 2001.

Obear, K.. "Best Practices That Address Homophobia and Heterosexism in Corporations." *Diversity Factor,* 2000, 9, 25–30.

Powers, B. "The Impact of Gay, Lesbian, and Bisexual Workplace Issues on Productivity." In A. Ellis and E. Riggle (eds.), *Sexual Identity on the Job: Issues and Services.* New York: Harrington Park Press/Hawthorn Press, 1996.

Ragins, B. R., and Cornwell, J. M. "Pink Triangles: Antecedents and Consequences of Perceived Workplace Discrimination Against Gay and Lesbian Employees." *Journal of Applied Psychology,* 2001, 86(6), 1244–1261.

Shaffer, D. R., and Wallace, A. "Belief Congruence and Evaluator Homophobia as Determinants of the Attractiveness of Component Homosexual and Heterosexual Males." *Journal of Psychology and Human Sexuality,* 1990, 3(1), 67–87.

Thomas, K. M. *Diversity Dynamics in the Workplace.* Belmont, Calif.: Wadsworth, 2005.

Thomas, K. M. (ed.). *Diversity Resistance.* Mahwah, N.J.: Erlbaum, forthcoming.

Wildman, S. A., and Davis, A. D. "Making Systems of Privilege Visible." In S. M. Wildman (ed.), *Privilege Revealed: How Invisible Preference Undermines America.* New York: New York University Press, 1995.

COREY S. MUÑOZ *is a research consultant for the Corporate Leadership Council in Washington D.C.*

KECIA M. THOMAS, *is a professor of psychology and African American studies at the University of Georgia and director of the Center for Research and Engagement in Diversity.*

9

This chapter highlights the major themes presented in this volume. It also offers a glimpse into LGBTQ issues in organizational settings that remain underrepresented in adult, continuing, and higher education.

Queer Challenges in Organizational Settings: Complexity, Paradox, and Contradiction

Robert J. Hill

The contemporary landscape is both diversified and diversifying; as such, LGBTQ presence is inevitable in organizational settings. The chapter authors in this volume sustain the assertions of a number of scholars (for example, Ahlstrom, 1999; Hill, 1995) that adult and continuing education efforts regarding LGBTQ issues are insufficient. A review of lesbian, gay, bisexual, and transgender issues in adult education by Kerka (2001) illustrates the dearth of scholarly products in the field. Fortunately, this is changing, at least for the lesbian and gay component of the equation.

Several key recurring themes emerge in this volume. Understanding the major leitmotivs will assist professionals in building safe and inclusive work and learning environments for adults related to sexual orientation, gender identity, and gender expression.

Avoiding Oversimplification

Many of the authors comment on the complexity, paradox, and contradiction surrounding contemporary discussions of sexual minorities. For example, King and Biro in Chapter Two propose a development model that highlights the multiple and intricate layers and various conflicts through which LGBTQ adults learn to navigate in their everyday lives in the workplace. Gedro in Chapter Four well illustrates the complicated nature of the topic and shows the interconnections among sexism, het-

NEW DIRECTIONS FOR ADULT AND CONTINUING EDUCATION, no. 112, Winter 2006 © 2006 Wiley Periodicals, Inc.
Published online in Wiley InterScience (www.interscience.wiley.com) • DOI: 10.1002/ace.240

erosexism, and homophobia. Lesbians in corporate America face multiple challenges, such as distinctive sexual identity development, unique sexual identity disclosure, prejudice (for being women and gay), and an often moralizing environment that affects success in their careers. Gedro calls attention to the triple bind that gay women of color face: heterosexism, sexism, and racism. In Chapter Six, Bettinger, one of the coauthors, also reminds us that multiply oppressed sexual minorities may face more difficult dilemmas when deciding to self-disclose than dominant group members do.

Tisdell, one of the coauthors of Chapter Six, introduces the question of representation. She reminds us that her own sexual orientation, like all other identity markers, cannot be easily categorized. This is the type of paradox found in this volume, which invites a postmodern reading. For example, the authors of Chapter Six comment on the fluid nature of "the closet" and challenge us to think deeply about what it means to be "out." Several of the chapter authors remind us that the world's many parts are not naturally or unimpeachably labeled. We are faced with the possibility that representing a sexual minority may inherently (and unwittingly) invite judging, evaluating, and interpreting the person by the one doing the representing. Tisdell's comments suggest that representing people by any label (lesbian, or bisexual, or straight, or closeted, for example) is a human endeavor and as such is value laden, partial, incomplete, and contingent. This volume invites us to ask whether the "discursive processes of naming, defining, [and] categorizing . . . subjects with seemingly coherent identities . . . are invented so as to permit their orderly disposition and governance" (Bryson and de Castell, 1993, p. 342), something that Foucault (1980) posits.

Silence and Invisibility: Adversaries of Inclusion

Another theme that emerges here is that the silence and invisibility of LGBTQ people in adult and continuing education, the business curriculum, higher education, and organizational settings reinforce stigmatization. Voice and visibility, critical change agents, are corollaries and thus have liberatory potential. If acceptance of difference is to occur, socialization of visible sexual minorities is a prerequisite (McMillan-Capehart, 2006). Gedro, for example, points out the necessity of visibility for lesbian role modeling. Grace and Wells report in Chapter Five that invisibility is perceived by sexual minority students and teachers as a tool of administrators and parents to thwart educational reform related to LGBTQ inclusion. The issue of visibility in a higher education setting is explored in Chapter Six, by Bettinger, Timmins, and Tisdell. They affirm that for them, the benefits of coming out, as seen from the location of the higher education classroom, exceeded the risks. Readers should note that context is critical.

New Directions for Adult and Continuing Education • DOI: 10.1002/ace

Homophobia and Heterosexism

All authors have much to say about homophobia and heterosexism. Chapter Three by Rocco and Gallagher is a major exposé of how homophobia and heterosexism work in organizations. Straight privilege is in the crosshairs of this chapter. Muñoz and Thomas (Chapter Eight) explore the various dimensions of discrimination that are elements of homophobia and heterosexism.

Career Killing

The lavender ceiling, a barrier to self-betterment for LGBTQ people in corporate and educational arenas, commands a central place in the work of various authors. It can be a career killer in many occupational settings, well beyond the U.S. military (arguably the largest provider of nonformal adult, and continuing education) where it is often an event made public.

Rocco and Gallagher in Chapter Three list behaviors and outcomes in the workplace that sidetrack career development. Their section on advancement is a conversation related to the lavender ceiling, discussed in Chapter One by Hill. In Chapter Seven, Hornsby shows how structures such as policies can encourage practices that either deny access to or enhance benefits for sexual minorities. The targets of these policies often differ from those who develop or approve them. This should give pause to those who elect to speak for the sexual other.

Diversity Education, Training, and Skills Development

Creating safe and productive environments, and strategies to value difference, should play key roles in organizational change for LGBTQ justice. Hornsby's work clearly illustrates the trends in organizational policies and practices and offers clear-cut guidelines for sensitizing individuals to the discriminatory effects of policies. Muñoz and Thomas in Chapter Eight, writing from the perspective of human resource development (HRD), remind us that continuous learning is necessary for personal and organizational transformation. Those familiar with the literature will recognize that Chapter Eight is one of only a few efforts to explore the intersection of HRD and sexual minority issues.

A few of the spaces where substantial learning will assist in building equality, mentioned by most authors in this volume, include (but are not limited to) policies, benefits, and networks:

- Institute nondiscrimination and antiharassment policies. Nearly all of the authors focus a concentrated beam of light on this theme. Hornsby and Muñoz and Thomas detail the importance of nondiscrimination and antiharassment policies as beginning steps in organizational best practices.

• Offer domestic partner benefits. This topic is at the fore of the cultural war of values that has consumed social discourse for more than a decade. In addition to these benefits in corporate settings, they should also be offered to adult students in higher education (Keeling and Schlapper, 1998), a topic seldom explored in the literature.

• Build and sustain networks and other support structures, and include allies (especially those who are influential in the organization) and ally groups.

Taboo Terrain: Transgender Notions

Several authors raise questions about transgender issues in the workplace. If managing a diverse workforce is central to organizational improvement, then addressing taboo issues, such as transgender people's rights, is a key component.

Lesbian Matters

The unique circumstances of lesbians are placed front and center by Gedro. She offers that lesbians are more disadvantaged than gay men in organizations because gay men have the potential to hide in the shadow of masculinity, which often dominates society and the workplace. She also reminds readers that self-disclosed lesbians are in the best position to reap the benefits of masculine stereotypes, which permit the putatively male behaviors of assertiveness productivity. King and Biro discuss in part issues specific to gay women's development. They offer a workplace scenario that illustrates lesbians' development concerns. Timmins, a coauthor of Chapter Six, adds to the rich narrative of lesbian experiences in the context of higher education. She reports that the energy and empowerment created by her personal life, and her growing political awareness and involvement, opened the way for liberation in an educational classroom that had been engineered for diversity.

The Subject of Struggle

Hostility and attempts to foil inclusivity—sometimes active and virulent, sometimes passive and symbolic—are unwelcome marks of LGBTQ success in organizational settings. Hornsby writes that visibility and publicity, such as gay pride marches, same-sex marriages and civil unions, child adoptions by sexual minorities, statutes barring sexual orientation discrimination, domestic partner benefits, and the popular media, are not only evidence of social change. They have also been catalysts for resistance and backlash. Muñoz and Thomas give insights into how organizational leaders can prepare for resistance.

New Directions for Adult and Continuing Education • DOI: 10.1002/ace

Fundamentalism and Moral/izing

Moral/izing is the process of applying moral codes, specific to a particular group of people, onto everyone. It is written here with a slash to illustrate the tensions and contradictions in being specific and generalized simultaneously. In adult education, a few attempts have been made to open discussions on the impacts of the moral/izing (in the context of the religious right wing) on the field. For example, the Third Annual Lesbian, Gay, Bisexual, Transgender, Queer, and Allies Caucus Pre-Conference of the 2005 Adult Education Research Conference (AERC) was titled "Hear Me Out: Queer Narratives, Moral/izing Discourses and the Academy." It proposed that moral/izing discourses characterize the present moment in much of the world and are deeply consequential for LGBTQ communities.

Engaging Adult Development

Kerka (2001) offers insight into the ways that adult development theories have been criticized for inadequately representing sexual orientation. The chapters in this volume by King and Biro, Rocco and Gallagher, and Gedro help to remedy this and are welcome additions to the development theories in adult education proposed by Edwards and Brooks (1999) and Resides (1996).

A significant question is how LGBTQ adults cope with and reconcile their personal journeys with their workplace climate. King and Biro offer that critical reflection and transformational learning build greater understanding of the LGBTQ self, our sexual identities, and societal expectations about us, and they open up the space and the freedom to question assumptions. These processes not only help us to understand ourselves, but also to understand the nonqueer other. Lesbian identity, and indirectly identity development, is excavated by Gedro. Here we encounter the notion that lesbians learn informally and incidentally in the workplace rather than primarily through attending classes, seminars, or other institutionally sponsored means. In higher education contexts, sexual identity development has been addressed by Sullivan (1998).

Conclusion

Queering organizations is a process that has gained some currency in the recent past. It is a complex practice with multiple dimensions and is fraught with paradox and contradiction. It can be a challenge to construct organizational climates that foster and value difference related to sexual orientation and gender identity. While organizations are not always liberatory locations for gay men, lesbians, bisexual, transgender, and self-identified queers, they can be shaped into welcoming environments that value diversity. To accomplish this, organizations need to gain knowledge, skills, tools, and resources to identify sexual minority needs, cultivate LGBTQ networks and ally groups,

New Directions for Adult and Continuing Education • DOI: 10.1002/ace

dismantle the lavender ceiling that prevents sexual minority mobility, interrogate heterosexual privilege and mount an assault on homophobia, design and implement nonharassment and antidiscrimination policies and practices, offer domestic partner benefits, and interpose best diversity practices (that include LGBTQ issues) into organizational strategies.

Fostering diversity can be rewarding to organizations that choose to do so. To be successful, organizations may have to realign structures and practices, implement new strategies of accountability, mobilize resources, and keep constant vigilance on their ultimate goal in order to sustain safe and productive environments for all members. When empowered to contribute to the vision and mission of organizations, sexual minorities are valuable assets vital to success. LGBTQ issues in adult, continuing, and higher education are key areas contributing to the kind of organizational change that reaps the vast rewards of diversity.

References

Ahlstrom, C. "Putting Lesbian and Gay Families in the Picture." In M. Merson and S. Reuys (eds.), *Taking Risks. Connections: A Journal of Adult Literacy.* Boston: Adult Literacy Resource Institute, Summer 1999.

Bryson, M., and de Castell, S. "En/Gendering Equity: On Some Paradoxical Consequences of Institutionalized Programs of Emancipation." *Educational Theory,* Winter 1993, *43*(3), 341–355.

Edwards, K., and Brooks, A. K. "The Development of Sexual Identity." In M. Carolyn Clark and R. S. Caffarella (eds.), *An Update on Adult Development Theory: New Ways of Thinking About the Life Course.* New Directions for Adult and Continuing Education, no. 84. San Francisco: Jossey-Bass, 1999.

Foucault, M. *Power/Knowledge: Selected Interviews and Other Writings, 1972–1977* (C. Gordon, ed.). New York: Pantheon Books, 1980.

Hill, R. J. "A Critique of Heterocentric Discourse in Adult Education: A Critical Review." *Adult Education Quarterly,* 1995, *45*(3), 142–158.

Keeling, R. P., and Schlapper, F. J. "Extending Benefits for Students' Domestic Partners." In R. L. Sanlo (ed.), *Working with Lesbian, Gay, Bisexual and Transgender College Students.* Westport, Conn.: Greenwood, 1998.

Kerka, S. (2001). "Adult Education and Gay, Lesbian, Bisexual, and Transgendered Communities." Trends and Issues Alert no. 21. Available from http://www.calpro-online.org/eric/docgen.asp?tbl=tia&ID=143. Accessed Jan. 23, 2006.

McMillan-Capehart, A. "Heterogeneity or Homogeneity: Socialization Makes the Difference When Diversity Is at Stake." *Performance Improvement Quarterly,* 2006, *19*(1), 83–99.

Resides, D. "Learning and New Voices: Lesbian Development and the Implications for Adult Education." In H. Reno and M. Witte (eds.), *Thirty-Seventh Annual Adult Education Research Conference Proceedings.* Tampa: University of South Florida, 1996.

Sullivan, P. L. "Sexual Identity Development: The Importance of Target or Dominant Group Membership." In R. L. Sanlo (ed.), *Working with Lesbian, Gay, Bisexual and Transgender College Students.* Westport, Conn.: Greenwood, 1998.

ROBERT J. HILL *is associate professor of adult education in the Department of Lifelong Education, Administration, and Policy at the University of Georgia, Athens.*

INDEX

Abalos, D., 66
ADA (Americans with Disabilities Act) [1990], 74, 81
Administrative affairs actions, 11
Adult education: creating inclusive environment for lesbians in, 47; gap in lesbian issues in, 41, 42-43. See also Classroom dilemmas; Higher education institutions
AERC LGBTQ & Allies Caucus, 13
AERC Pre-Conference (2005), 101
AERC (Thirty-Fourth Adult Education Research Conference), 8
Affinity groups, 90-91
African Americans, 30
Agape (Canada), 57-58
Age Discrimination in Employment Act (1967), 74
Ahlstrom, C., 97
Alberta Individual Rights Protection Act (Canada), 54
Alberta Teachers' Association (ATA), 54
Alberta, Vriend v., 53-54
Alderson, K. G., 31, 42
Alexander, J., 65
Allen, K. R., 9, 32, 34
Altman, D., 14
American Association of Retired Persons, 73
Americans with Disabilities Act (ADA) [1990], 74, 81
Armstrong, M., 32
ATA Declaration of Rights and Responsibilities for Teachers (Canada), 54

Backlash, 12-13
Becky's perspective, 65-66
Behavioral protection actions, 11
Bettinger, T. V., 2, 63, 66-70, 98
Bierema, L., 43
Biro, S. C., 1, 17, 27, 101
Bisexuality, 3
Black, D., 44
Blandford, J., 45, 47
Board of the Society for Human Resource Management, 10
Boatwright, K. J., 31, 35, 42
Borow, H., 33

Bowers v. Hardwick, 75
Brindley, R., 55
Brooks, A. K., 19, 22, 25, 26, 101
Brown, L. S., 43, 44, 45
Bryson, M., 98
Building Safe, Caring, and Inclusive Schools for LGBT Students (Canada), 59
Bullying (workplace), 75-76
Bumiller, E., 12
Button, S. B., 36, 43, 92

Canada: action planning to transform school culture in, 56-59; inclusion lacking in school culture of, 54-56; marginalization of sexual minorities in, 51-53; preservice teacher education in, 58; Quebec Provincial Law-Labour Standards, 76; representative progress in law/policy in, 53-54
Canada, Egan and Nesbit v., 53
Canadian Charter of Rights and Freedoms, 52, 53
Canadian Human Rights Act, 75
Canadian Human Rights Commission, 74
Canadian Teachers' Federation, 52, 53
Career: advancement of, 35-36; choosing employment and, 34; definition of, 33; establishment of, 34-35; management of, 36; segmented processes of, 33-34; work/life roles affected by, 36
Career construction theory, 33
Career development: deconstructing straight privilege in, 34-36; heterosexism privilege in, 30, 86-87; how sexual identity interweaves with stages of, 24-25; lavender ceiling and, 10, 99; moral/izing and discrimination issues in, 29, 30-31, 101; queering, 29, 36-37; research and theoretical development on, 33-34; role models for lesbians and, 48; social distancing impact on, 87
Career development theory, 33-34
Carlin, D., 47
Cas, V., 44
Cass, V., 18

103

Back Issue/Subscription Order Form

Copy or detach and send to:

Jossey-Bass, A Wiley Imprint, 989 Market Street, San Francisco, CA 94103-1741
Call or fax toll-free: Phone 888-378-2537 6:30AM – 3PM PST; Fax 888-481-2665

Back Issues: Please send me the following issues at $29 each
(Important: please include series initials and issue number, such as ACE96.)

_____

_____

_____

$ _____   Total for single issues

$ _____   SHIPPING CHARGES: SURFACE   Domestic   Canadian

		Domestic	Canadian
First Item		$5.00	$6.00
Each Add'l Item		$3.00	$1.50

For next-day and second-day delivery rates, call the number listed above.

Subscriptions: Please __start __renew my subscription to *New Directions for Adult and Continuing Education* for the year 2_____ at the following rate:

U.S.	__Individual $80	__Institutional $195
Canada	__Individual $80	__Institutional $235
All Others	__Individual $104	__Institutional $269

For more information about online subscriptions visit
www.interscience.wiley.com

$ _____   Total single issues and subscriptions (Add appropriate sales tax for your state for single issue orders. No sales tax for U.S. subscriptions. Canadian residents, add GST for subscriptions and single issues.)

__Payment enclosed (U.S. check or money order only)
__VISA __MC __AmEx #_____ Exp. Date _____

Signature _____ Day Phone _____
__ Bill me (U.S. institutional orders only. Purchase order required.)

Purchase order # _____
         Federal Tax ID13559302   **GST 89102 8052**

Name _____

Address _____

_____

Phone _____ E-mail _____

For more information about Jossey-Bass, visit our Web site at www.josseybass.com

would argue that it requires intentional action, a willingness to take personal risk, a genuine concern for the learners' betterment, and the wherewithal to draw on a variety of methods and techniques that help create a classroom environment that encourages and supports personal growth. What makes the work of transformative learning even more difficult is the lack of clear signposts or guidelines that teachers can follow when they try to teach for change. There is now a need to return to the classroom and look through the lens of those who have been engaged in the practice of fostering transformative learning. This volume's authors are seasoned practitioners and scholars who have grappled with the fundamental issues associated with teaching for change (emotion, expressive ways of knowing, power, cultural difference, context, teacher authenticity, spirituality) in a formal classroom setting; introduced innovations that enhance the practice of fostering transformative learning; and asked ethical questions that need to be explored and reflected upon when practicing transformative learning in the classroom.
ISBN 0-7879-8584-8

ACE108 Adulthood: New Terrain

Mary Alice Wolf

One of the many surprises about the lifespan perspective is that individuals, families, institutions, and corporations lead *many* lives. The purpose of this resource is to acquaint and update practitioners in adult education and related roles with emerging and creative methods of 1) appreciating the learner's perspective, 2) moderating content and learning format to enhance meaning-making in the learning environment, and 3) developing tools to address alternative modes of development and growth that occur in adulthood and challenge adult educators on a daily basis.

What does the new adult learner look like? This volume contains theory and research on learners who turn to educational programs in times of transition and explores ways of connecting with new cognitive and affective meanings.

This volume explores dimensions of adult development from ethnographic, research, and theoretical perspectives. It addresses adult learners' experience and meaning of education as an ongoing resource for well-being and positive development across the lifecourse. It updates the reader in the emerging terrain of adulthood; adult learning philosophies are implemented and modified to meet adults' developmental mandate to continue learning in order to make meaning and find purpose during the countless transitions of the ever-increasing adult years.
ISBN 0-7879-8396-0

ACE107 Artistic Ways of Knowing: Expanded Opportunities for Teaching and Learning

Randee Lipson Lawrence

This volume of *New Directions for Adult and Continuing Education* challenges the dominant paradigm of how knowledge is typically constructed and shared in adult education settings by focusing on ways in which adult educators can expand learning opportunities and experiences for their learners. Art appeals universally to us all and has the capacity to bridge cultural differences. Art can also foster individual and social transformation, promoting dialogue and deepening awareness of ourselves and the world around us. The contributors to this volume include actors, musicians,

photographers, storytellers, and poets, all of whom also happen to be adult educators. In each chapter, the author describes how one or more forms of artistic expression were used to promote learning in formal or informal adult education settings. In each case, the purpose of education was not to teach art (that is, not to develop expertise in acting, poetry writing, or creating great works of art). Conversely, art was used as a means to access learning in subjects as divergent as English language acquisition, action research, community awareness, and social justice.
ISBN 0-7879-8284-9

ACE106 Class Concerns: Adult Education and Social Class
Tom Nesbitt
This volume of *New Directions for Adult and Continuing Education* brings together several leading progressive adult educators to explore how class affects different arenas of adult education practice and discourse. It highlights the links between adult education, the material and social conditions of daily and working lives, and the economic and political systems that underpin them. Chapters focus on adult education policies; teaching; learning and identity formation; educational institutions and social movements; and the relationships between class, gender, and race. Overall, the volume reaffirms the salience of class in shaping the lives we lead and the educational approaches we develop. It offers suggestions for adult educators to identify and resist the encroachments of global capitalism and understand the role of education in promoting social equality. Finally, it suggests that a class perspective can provide an antidote to much of the social amnesia, self-absorption, and apolitical theorizing that pervades current adult education discourse.
ISBN 0-7879-8128-1

ACE105 HIV/AIDS Education for Adults
John P. Egan
Contributors from the United States, Canada, and Australia, working in university-based and community-based environments and for divergent communities—present specific experiences in the fight against HIV/AIDS. They share stories of shifting paradigms and challenging norms, and of seeking and finding innovation. Topics examined include the struggle for meaning and power in HIV/AIDS education, HIV prevention workers and injection drug users, community-based research, grassroots response to HIV/AIDS in Nova Scotia, sex workers and HIV/AIDS education, and the Tuskegee Syphilis Study and legacy recruitment for experimental vaccines. By examining HIV/AIDS through an adult education lens, we gain insights into how communities (and governments) can respond quickly and effectively to emergent health issues—and other issues linked to marginalization.
ISBN 0-7879-8032-3

ACE104 Embracing and Enhancing the Margins of Adult Education
Meg Wise, Michelle Glowacki-Dudka
Adult educators increasingly risk and resist being placed at the margins of academic and other organizations. This volume argues that depending on how those margins are defined, margins can be a place of creativity and power from which to examine and challenge dominant ideology and practice. Chapters explore advances and effective practices being made in the margins of adult education from several perspectives including

community-based programs, interreligious learning, human resource development, African American underrepresentation in the academy, and degree granting adult education programs. Other areas explored include an interdisciplinary Web-based patient education research program and educational focus on citizenship and public responsibility skills.
ISBN 0-7879-7859-0

ACE103 Developing and Delivering Adult Degree Programs
James P. Pappas, Jerry Jerman
The explosive growth in adult degree programs is fueled by increased distance education technologies, potential for providing additional revenue streams for institutions, fierce competition from the private sector and from other higher education institutions, and rising interest in interdisciplinary programs. This issue explores adult degree programs and considers the theoretical underpinnings of such programs and hands-on issues as curriculum, faculty, marketing, technology, financing, and accreditation, all with a goal of informing and equipping both scholars and practitioners.
ISBN 0-7879-7767-5

ACE102 Promoting Critical Practice in Adult Education
Ralf St. Clair, Jennifer A. Sandlin
The idea that critical perspectives on teaching are difficult to enact in the classrooms is not new. And what do we mean by *critical perspectives* anyway? In this volume some of the most exciting scholars in adult education—whether established or emerging—provide insights into what it means to be critical and how it affects the concrete practices of teaching adults. Chapter topics include critical theory, feminism, critical postmodernism, Africentrism, queer theory, and cultural studies.
ISBN 0-7879-7590-7

ACE101 Adult Education in an Urban Context: Problems, Practices, and Programming for Inner-City Communities
Larry G. Martin, Elice E. Rogers
This sourcebook offers adult education scholars and practitioners in academic, community, and work-related urban settings insight into the education and learning problems and needs confronted by low-income residents of inner-city communities. Additionally, it offers fresh perspectives and approaches to practice that can assist these residents in crossing the socioeconomic and race-ethnicity borders that separate them from more affluent urban communities.
ISBN 0-7879-7433-1

ACE100 Facilitating Learning in Online Environments
Steven R. Aragon
Presents models, methods, and strategies that facilitate and promote learning within online environments. Arguing that success in online environments is dependent on the role of autonomy in order to create sustained and enduring learners, contributors demonstrate how quality online programs are made up of a "blend" of technology, pedagogy, organization, strategy, and vision; explore the concept of online social presence as a significant factor in improving instructional effectiveness and contributing to a feeling of community among learners; and offer strategies for instructors facing the new challenges and opportunities of the online educational experience.
ISBN 0-7879-7268-1

United States Postal Service

Statement of Ownership, Management, and Circulation

1. Publication Title	2. Publication Number								3. Filing Date
New Directions For Adult & Continuing Education	1	0	5	2	_	2	8	9	1	10/1/06

4. Issue Frequency	5. Number of Issues Published Annually	6. Annual Subscription Price
Quarterly	4	$195.00

7. Complete Mailing Address of Known Office of Publication (Not printer) (Street, city, county, state, and ZIP+4)	Contact Person Joe Schuman
Wiley Subscription Services, Inc. at Jossey-Bass, 989 Market Street, San Francisco, CA 94103	Telephone (415) 782-3232

8. Complete Mailing Address of Headquarters or General Business Office of Publisher (Not printer)

Wiley Subscription Services, Inc. 111 River Street, Hoboken, NJ 07030

9. Full Names and Complete Mailing Addresses of Publisher, Editor, and Managing Editor (Do not leave blank)

Publisher (Name and complete mailing address)

Wiley Subscriptions Services, Inc., A Wiley Company at San Francisco, 989 Market Street, San Francisco, CA 94103-1741

Editor (Name and complete mailing address)

Susan Imel, Ohio State University/Eric-Acve, 1900 Kenny Road, Columbus, OH 43210-1090

Managing Editor (Name and complete mailing address)

None

10. Owner (Do not leave blank. If the publication is owned by a corporation, give the name and address of the corporation immediately followed by the names and addresses of all stockholders owning or holding 1 percent or more of the total amount of stock. If not owned by a corporation, give the names and addresses of the individual owners. If owned by a partnership or other unincorporated firm, give its name and address as well as those of each individual owner. If the publication is published by a nonprofit organization, give its name and address.)

Full Name	Complete Mailing Address
Wiley Subscription Services, Inc.	111 River Street, Hoboken, NJ 07030
(see attached list)	

11. Known Bondholders, Mortgagees, and Other Security Holders Owning or Holding 1 Percent or More of Total Amount of Bonds, Mortgages, or Other Securities. If none, check box   → ☑ None

Full Name	Complete Mailing Address
None	None

12. Tax Status (For completion by nonprofit organizations authorized to mail at nonprofit rates) (Check one)
The purpose, function, and nonprofit status of this organization and the exempt status for federal income tax purposes:
☐ Has Not Changed During Preceding 12 Months
☐ Has Changed During Preceding 12 Months (Publisher must submit explanation of change with this statement)

13. Publication Title New Directions For Adult & Continuing Education	14. Issue Date for Circulation Data Below Summer 2006

15.		Extent and Nature of Circulation	Average No. Copies Each Issue During Preceding 12 Months	No. Copies of Single Issue Published Nearest to Filing Date
a.		Total Number of Copies (Net press run)	1445	1456
b. Paid and/or Requested Circulation	(1)	Paid/Requested Outside-County Mail Subscriptions Stated on Form 3541. (Include advertiser's proof and exchange copies)	481	471
	(2)	Paid In-County Subscriptions Stated on Form 3541 (Include advertiser's proof and exchange copies)	0	0
	(3)	Sales Through Dealers and Carriers, Street Vendors, Counter Sales, and Other Non-USPS Paid Distribution	0	0
	(4)	Other Classes Mailed Through the USPS	0	0
c.		Total Paid and/or Requested Circulation [Sum of 15b. (1), (2),(3),and (4)] ▶	481	471
d. Free Distribution by Mail (Samples, complimentary, and other free)	(1)	Outside-County as Stated on Form 3541	0	0
	(2)	In-County as Stated on Form 3541	0	0
	(3)	Other Classes Mailed Through the USPS	0	0
e.		Free Distribution Outside the Mail (Carriers or other means)	68	67
f.		Total Free Distribution (Sum of 15d. and 15e.) ▶	68	67
g.		Total Distribution (Sum of 15c. and 15f) ▶	549	538
h.		Copies not Distributed	896	918
i.		Total (Sum of 15g. and h.) ▶	1445	1456
j.		Percent Paid and/or Requested Circulation (15c. divided by 15g. times 100)	88%	88%

16. Publication of Statement of Ownership
☑ Publication required. Will be printed in the Winter 2006 issue of this publication.   ☐ Publication not required.

17. Signature and Title of Editor, Publisher, Business Manager, or Owner		Date
Susan E. Lewis, VP & Publisher - Periodicals	_Susan Lewis_	10/01/06

I certify that all information furnished on this form is true and complete. I understand that anyone who furnishes false or misleading information on this form or who omits material or information requested on the form may be subject to criminal sanctions (including fines and imprisonment) and/or civil sanctions (including civil penalties).